A Guide To California's Freshwater Fishes

by
Bob Madgic

Illustrated by
William L. Crary

Naturegraph Publishers

Library of Congress Cataloging-in-Publication Data

Madgic, Bob.
    A guide to California's freshwater fishes / by Bob
Madgic; illustrated by William L. Crary.
        p. cm.
    ISBN 0-87961-254-1
    1. Freshwater Fishes—California—Identification.
2. Freshwater fishes—California—Pictorial works. I.
Title.
QL628.C2M245 1999
597.176'09794—dc21   98-32180
                                                         CIP

ISBN 0-87961-254-1

Copyright © 1999
by Bob Madgic and William L. Crary

2001 printing

Cover fish—largemouth bass, California golden
trout (state fish), and summer steelhead—and all
other paintings and art work by William L. Crary

Photo credits shown with photo.
Back cover photo by Samuel V. Johnson.

Naturegraph Publishers has been publishing books
on natural history, Native Americans, and outdoor
subjects since 1946. Please write for our free catalog.

Books for a better world

Naturegraph Publishers, Inc.
3543 Indian Creek Road
Happy Camp, CA 96039
(530) 493-5353

Table of Contents

List of Illustrations

(Excluding fish paintings)

Photos

Maps and Diagrams

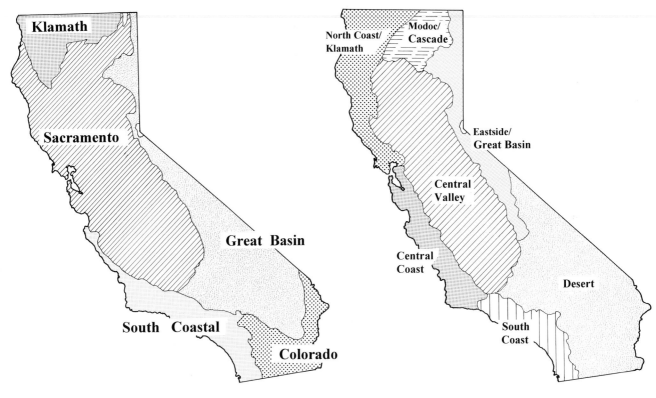

Fish Provinces of California.

River Regions of California.

Introduction

Fish are vital creatures in the web of life, sources of food for people, mammals and birds, objects of recreation for countless individuals, and the basis for millions of jobs. As the most important indicator of aquatic diversity, fish tell us about the health of our waterways, our environment, and ultimately our planet.

For those whose livelihoods or recreational activities depend on fish, the preservation of this resource is indeed important. But each of us has a stake in the well-being of California's fishes. It is important for us all to be informed about these creatures and the places where they live.

The purpose of this guidebook is to assist anyone interested in the natural world—students, anglers, outdoor enthusiasts—to identify and learn more about the fish species inhabiting California's waters. It traces the history of California's freshwater fish populations, from the state's precious but long threatened native species to the many introduced species now dominating the Golden State's innumerable rivers, streams, lakes, and reservoirs. In many respects, California's history is reflected in the changing status of its fishes.

A Guide to California's Freshwater Fishes informs the reader on the importance of preserving native fish species. It identifies requisite habitat for sustaining a fishery, includes ways for categorizing fish, and presents data such as angling records for respective game fish. It summarizes recent activities and reports of fish biologists and governmental agencies responsible for managing fish, in particular the California Department of Fish and Game.

The magnificence of California's fishes is readily apparent from their own visual images. *A Guide to California's Freshwater Fishes* presents detailed illustrations and information on each fish species and significant subspecies. Generally cast in non-technical language, this book is intended for the lay person.

An estuary–important fish habitat. Photo by Pat Higgins.

Ways to Group Fish

Freshwater fish can be grouped according to several distinctions that help in identifications and decisions on fish management. The following represent the most important groupings:

Species: A distinct population of fish that interbreeds in nature, and does not breed with members of other populations. A population is considered "distinct" if it represents an evolutionary significant unit of the biological species.

Subspecies: A category of fish genetically distinguishable from other categories within the same species, and capable of interbreeding with them.

Race: A grouping of a subspecies of fish with similar behavioral characteristics.

Strain: A grouping of fish possessing common ancestry and clear-cut physiological characteristics (due to its environment for instance) but which do not have a unique morphological (physical) structure causing it to be considered a separate subspecies or species.

* * *

Native: A fish species indigenous to its environment, often representing millions of years of evolutionary development. (Due to its genetic makeup and adaptation to its natural environment, a native species is the most significant and valuable member of an ecosystem.)

Introduced: A fish species not native to the waterway but one introduced to it through unnatural processes, e.g. actions by man. Such non-native or "alien" species can disrupt the natural balance within an ecosystem.

* * *

Wild Fish: A free-living fish, hatched and reared in a stream, lake, or sea from an egg spawned and deposited there by its mother, and which has successfully adapted to its environment. (Wild fish need not be native creatures as in the cases of brown and brook trout.)

Hatchery-Reared or Stocked: Fish spawned in a hatchery and maintained there by humans until placed in a natural waterway. Hatchery fish are planted in waters, sometimes as fingerlings or fry (very small fish), or as catchable-sized.

* * *

Resident: Fish residing in the water where they were spawned, usually in a limited section of river or stream. Residents in freshwater streams and lakes live their entire lives in fresh water.

Anadromous: Fish that live in both fresh and salt waters. The young fish, hatched in fresh water, migrate to the sea, where they grow into adult specimens. They return to fresh water, usually, but not always, for spawning purposes.

* * *

Coldwater Species: In general, coldwater fish require aquatic habitats with temperatures below 68° F, high oxygen content, and good water clarity.

Warmwater Species: Fish capable of surviving conditions of higher temperature, e.g. 80° F, lower oxygen, high turbidity, and mud bottoms.

Note: River habitats vary beyond the two general types summarized above. Further, some fish species are distributed over several habitats, and occupy transitional environments between the coldwater and warmwater types. Anadromous species must be able to live in many different habitats.

* * *

Game Fish: Fish pursued by sportsmen for recreational purposes, or for their food value. In California, trout are the most sought after game fish, representing about sixty percent of freshwater angling. The second most popular is black bass, accounting for twelve percent of angling demand. The third most popular game fish is catfish. Behind trout, the fish caught the most belong to the group generally called "panfish," which includes the sunfishes (excluding largemouth and smallmouth bass), yellow perch, and crappie.

Non-Game Fish: Fish not possessing recreational or food value for humans.

California Freshwater Fishes: A Brief History

California's Coldwater Natives: At one time California possessed one of the world's richest freshwater fisheries. Each year millions of salmon migrated up the state's innumerable rivers and streams to spawn. They included chinook or king salmon, coho or silver salmon, chum, pink, and occasionally sockeye salmon. Another ocean-run fish, the anadromous rainbow trout, now called *steelhead* for their steel blue topside, fought their way up crashing waterways, often reaching the headwaters of pristine mountain rivers and streams. The abundant salmon and steelhead populations provided Native Americans with a staple food source, and a foundation for their culture.

The ocean wasn't the only source for this natural bounty. In California's inland waters resided some of the most beautiful fish imaginable—the state's native trout species. They included: Lahontan cutthroat trout, coastal cutthroat trout, Paiute cutthroat trout, coastal rainbow trout (the seagoing race known as steelhead), Kern River rainbow trout, Eagle Lake rainbow trout, Volcano Creek golden trout, Little Kern golden trout, McCloud River redband trout, Goose Lake redband trout, Warner Valley redband trout, and the bull trout. With the exception of Lahontan cutthroat that California shared with Nevada, bull trout that were abundant throughout northwestern states, Goose Lake and Warner Valley redbands that also lived in Oregon waters, and coastal cutthroat and steelhead whose boundaries extended all the way to Alaska, these trout were unique to California, collectively representing major contributions to North American fisheries.

Each of the above trout possessed its own evolutionary niche. Consider the Lahontan cutthroat, the largest trout in North America. This fish regularly grew up to sixty pounds in its native, unspoiled environment. Tens of thousands of them, many over thirty pounds, migrated each spring from Pyramid and Walker lakes in Nevada, up rivers and streams of the eastern Sierra Nevada, principally the Truckee and Walker rivers. Nowhere else in the world has there been a native trout fishery comparable to that of the Lahontan cutthroat.

In the alkaline waters of Eagle Lake, another robust trout evolved and flourished—the Eagle Lake rainbow. And tucked away in alpine waters, our most beautiful trout subspecies existed: the Paiute cutthroat, the Volcano Creek golden, the Little Kern golden, and the Kern River rainbow.

California's coastal rainbow trout represents one of the world's greatest fishes. The steelhead has not only been a legendary sporting fish in California, but its eggs have been sent to the far reaches of the globe, creating the renowned rainbow fisheries in New Zealand and Argentina. Less conspicuous in coastal waters was the coastal cutthroat, a fish that resembles the rainbow and behaves like salmon and steelhead by spending time in salt water and migrating up coastal streams to spawn.

Steelhead gave rise to the rare McCloud River redband trout, another strikingly beautiful subspecies of rainbow that evolved upstream of geological barriers, separating it for eons from its anadromous ancestor. Downsteam in the icy McCloud River resided a singularly predacious fish—the bull trout. And in the mountainous regions of northeastern California lived the Goose Lake and Warner Valley redband trout, capable of living in warmer waters than their rainbow cousins.

California was also home to a unique carryover from prehistoric times—the sturgeon. These ancient fish, representing millions of years of evolutionary development and survival, and sometimes a century in age, migrated from the ocean up northern California rivers.

Unbelievably, human ignorance, greed, and neglect have almost destroyed California's native salmonid fishery. The bull trout is extinct in California. The Lahontan cutthroat came close to extinction, as have the Paiute cutthroat, the Little Kern golden, the Kern River rainbow, and the redband. Steelhead are absent from or extremely scarce in rivers where they formerly thrived in abundance. Numbers of coastal cutthroat have declined. Even runs of the mighty salmon have been nearly eliminated from many California rivers, and the sturgeon population was almost exhausted at one time.

Freshwater fish species are in serious trouble. Of the 116 native California fishes, over two-thirds are considered *species of special concern* (a state designation), including a number already extinct or extirpated from their native waters. Sixty-six of these native fish are found only in California, including the Sacramento perch, the Clear Lake hitch, the tule perch, and varied subspecies of pupfish, stickleback, chub, suckers, dace, lamprey, sculpin, and roach. These declines have been due to widespread destruction of habitat required by fish. The indiscriminate introduction of alien fish species also proved disastrous to many of California's native fishes.

Middle Falls on the upper McCloud River. Photo by Bob Madgic.

Fish Introductions. While the habitats of native fish were being thoroughly degraded, man was bringing new fish species into the state, many of which dominate California's waters today. With the exception of Florida, no state has introduced more alien fish species than California.

Fish introductions began in the second half of the nineteenth century primarily as potential new food sources. In June 1871, the California Fish Commission (the forerunner of the Department of Fish and Game) arranged for the transport of 10,000 American shad from the East Coast, where they were considered an outstanding food fish, and placed them into the Sacramento River. The shad successfully navigated to the Pacific Ocean, returning to the Sacramento each year to spawn. Californians generally didn't develop a taste for the flesh of American shad, but the fish eventually became an important game fish. The importation of striped bass from the East Coast followed in 1879, again as a food fish. It, too, later developed into a prized game fish.

Two trout species destined to impact the future of trout in California entered the state around this time: the brook trout (1871), and the brown trout (1893). Less significant was the lake trout, placed in Lake Tahoe in 1895. Before the nineteenth century ended, varied government agencies and private groups had introduced many additional warmwater fish, including catfish, black bass, smallmouth bass, carp, yellow perch, green sunfish, white and black crappie, and warmouth. Introductions of bluegill and pumpkinseed followed in 1908 and 1918 respectively. Except for the trout species, the basis for these introductions was their food potentials. Sporting values surfaced later, as did the practices of experimentation and "acclimatization" for their own sake. The fish gurus of the day believed that it was in the country's best interests to stock any promising fish species in any water. One example difficult to explain was the (unsuccessful) attempt to introduce Atlantic salmon to California's waters, already rich with Pacific salmon.

In the mid 1930s, the California Department of Fish and Game (DFG) began to question the impact of fish introductions on the state's native species and the wisdom of doing any more. Experimentation often had unknown and detrimental consequences. Once a species got established in certain waters (e.g. the bullhead in Sierra Nevada lakes), it was almost impossible to eradicate. Some alien species brought about the demise of native species in many waters. For example, the bluegill proved too competitive for the native Sacramento perch when placed in the same waters, leading to the extirpation of the perch from its home waters. The voracious lake trout was partially responsible for the elimination of the Lahontan cutthroat from Lake Tahoe by consuming the young cutthroat fish. Nonetheless, many introduced species were irreversibly established in many waters.

For the next couple of decades, new introductions were only done to fill a particular niche, such as planting spotted bass and kokanee salmon in waters where other species did not prosper. The DFG reversed this more prudent policy when California began constructing more reservoirs, which are usually more conducive to warmwater fishes.

Dams and Reservoirs. Although large irrigation reservoirs first appeared in California in 1859, the state had only about 35,000 acres of impounded water by 1940, and most of these were in southern California. By 1950, the acreage of reservoirs doubled to about 70,000 acres. Then, with the state's population exploding, so too did demands for water to support housing and commercial developments, especially in the semi-arid south. By 1983, California's water storage had increased five-fold to about 350,000 acres. Despite the state's increasing urbanization and water storage, agriculture continued to consume its allotted eighty percent of the state's water supplies.

Many of California's prime waterways had been sacrificed to dams, principally the result of the massive federal Central Valley Project (CVP) that sent northern California water south. These structures prevented anadromous fish from reaching their spawning waters. Water diversions further deprived fish of precious water to spawn and grow. In addition, about ninety-four percent of the freshwater wetlands of the Central Valley, wetlands that at one time furnished spawning and nursery acreage for many fish, had been destroyed. The Californian landscape had been permanently changed.

With the ready availability of new, large bodies of water, increasing numbers of anglers sought them out to fish. (California has thousands of small lakes, mainly in mountain regions, but few large natural lakes.) Meanwhile, dams on some rivers enhanced coldwater fisheries by creating tailwaters—stretches of river dependent upon dam releases for their flows. Some of the best trout rivers in the state today are tailwaters that provide constant, cold water flows all season long through releases from the bottom of the reservoir, thereby producing a reliable environment for aquatic organisms. Such tailwaters include the Sacramento River below Shasta Lake, the East Walker below Bridgeport Reservoir, the Middle Fork of the Stanislaus below Beardsley Reservoir, the

Shasta Lake is California's largest reservoir. Photo by Diane Madgic.

McCloud below Lake McCloud, and Bear Creek below Big Bear Lake. (Other types of waterways are spring-fed creeks that receive most of their water from voluminous underground springs, e.g. Hat Creek, Fall River; and freestone rivers that are tumbling waters consisting mainly of snow melt and surface runoff, e.g. the East Carson, the Kern.) On the other hand, dams thoroughly degraded formerly outstanding cold-water fisheries such as the Pit and the North Fork of the Feather rivers. In these cases, a series of dams on each river significantly reduced flows and provided for erratic releases, producing extended periods of warm water more conducive to competing non-game fish, such as suckers and squawfish, than trout. (The management of one section in the Pit River below Lake Britton is providing for greater and more consistent flows, reestablishing productive trout water there once again.)

More Introductions. At mid-century the Department of Fish and Game again started emphasizing fish introductions and plantings in new waters. Its stated objective in 1951 was "to supply the best possible fishing for the greatest number of anglers." Under this new orthodoxy, fish existed basically for man's purposes. The State began eliminating non-game fish, such as suckers and squawfish, through chemical treatments of selected streams, lakes, and reservoirs. In 1952-54, for instance, over 250 miles of the Russian River and its tributaries were chemically treated to purge the water of non-game fish.

To keep up with angling demands, state biologists once more sought new game fish for California. In the fifties, the DFG introduced Florida largemouth bass and the redeye bass to some waters. One of the most controversial introductions was the white bass, a predacious freshwater fish. In 1965, 160 fingerlings were planted in Nacimiento Reservoir, San Luis Obispo County, to provide anglers with a game fish that would also feed on threadfin shad, an introduced forage fish becoming too numerous. The white bass thrived in what was thought to be a restricted body of water. However, a few anglers illegally transported live white bass to Lake Kaweah, a lake that sometimes overflowed. When it did, fish could enter Tulare Lake basin from which farmers pumped excess water into the North Fork of the Kings River, a tributary to the San Joaquin. By thus having access to the Delta, the white bass could threaten striped bass and chinook salmon populations, and important aquatic resources of the Central Valley. The DFG aggressively poisoned waters the white bass might have entered. This incident, still an open issue, points to the naivete of fish managers who believed a fish species could be confined to specific waters despite their well-known ability to escape, or the ease with which individuals could transport fish to other waters. Even exotic aquarium fish such as goldfish and mollies were routinely placed in wild waters where they established homes.

Some introductions of foreign species proved beneficial. One example is the Alabama spotted bass. Needed was a species of black bass capable of spawning and maintaining its population in reservoirs where water levels fluctuated and organic habitat deteriorated, leaving a predominantly barren rocky substrate when the reservoir level dropped. Alabama spotted bass met these criteria since they spawn in deeper water and in a more open or barren substrate. Plus they grow rapidly and live long lives, thus providing a richer sport fishery than other black bass subspecies. Introduced in 1974 in Perris Lake in Riverside County, the Alabama spotted bass has since been stocked in many reservoirs throughout the state to the delight of anglers.

The ongoing practice of introductions, designed to enhance sporting opportunities, led to increasingly artificial environments and fishing experiences. Angling in California became more and more designed, and less and less natural. A reliance on hatchery-produced fish soon became the norm.

Hatcheries. In 1872 the Federal Fish Commission established a hatchery on the McCloud River to gather the eggs of chinook salmon for exportation back east to replace vanishing Atlantic salmon from New England streams. In the following decades, varied state, federal, and private agencies launched hatcheries up and down the state primarily to hatch and rear fingerling trout, salmon, and steelhead. The State planted brook, rainbow, and brown trout in a myriad of waters, including many alpine lakes where no fish had previously existed and where brookies did exceptionally well. Little concern existed for how these plants impacted native trout and the natural world.

When it was learned a small percentage of hatchery fingerlings actually survived, particularly those stocked in streams, and that those that did were failing to meet the growing demands of anglers, the State started planting "catchable-sized" trout, e.g. six to ten inches, in the early 1930s. Thus began the concept of raising fish artificially and placing them in waters for the instant gratification of the fishing public, that is, "put and take" fishing. Fishing ponds for kids epitomized this artificial environment.

The Wildlife Conservation Act of 1949 laid the foundation for the modern hatchery system. Its purpose was to fill the void between anglers' demands

Lake Piru, north of Los Angeles, is typical of Southern California water storage reservoirs with its steep canyon sides. Photo by Richard Alden Bean.

and nature's ability to produce. Since fish grew faster in warmer waters, as demonstrated by the Hot Creek Trout Hatchery in Mono County constructed in 1941, some hatcheries located near cold water closed, and several new ones opened. Sixteen hatcheries were soon carrying out the new emphasis of supplying hatchery trout to the state's waters with the objective of making popular fish species so abundant that catch regulations would be unnecessary. (Currently California operates twenty hatcheries. Of these, twelve are trout hatcheries and eight are salmon and steelhead hatcheries. There is one federal salmon and steelhead hatchery in the state. Plus, many private fish farms rear fish, including a few warmwater species.)

The combination of large reservoirs, fish introductions, and hatchery-reared fish, led to bodies of water up and down the state holding a wide variety of game fish. For instance, no fewer than these fifteen game fish species exist in the largest reservoir in the state, Shasta Lake: chinook salmon, rainbow trout, brown trout, largemouth bass, smallmouth bass, Alabama spotted bass, black bullhead, brown bullhead (rare), white catfish, channel catfish, green sunfish, bluegill, black crappie, white crappie (rare), and white sturgeon (rare). Numerous non-game fish also swim the lake's waters. Many other reservoirs across the state contain several species of coldwater and warmwater game fish, although not as wide an assortment as Shasta's.

The Federal Endangered Species Act. By the 1970s, understandings about ecosystems and the importance of biodiversity came to the fore, spurred by reports from scientists, university professors, and leading environmental agencies and organizations. ("Biodiversity" refers to the myriad of plant and animal species throughout nature, the genetic variability among species, and the interlocking web of life. When any species disappears, its absence may trigger the demise of other species, possibly causing extinctions to snowball, thus leading to simpler and simpler cultures more prone to catastrophic losses. The more varied and complex a culture, i.e. the more varied and numerous the species within it, the greater stability it possesses, and the more adaptable it is to change.) Public concerns were growing about the numbers of species already extinct and approaching extinction, and the consequences to humankind and the earth. (Harvard University biologist E. O. Wilson has estimated that, worldwide, more than 50,000 species die out each year, or 136 species a day.) In response, Congress passed the Federal Endangered Species Act (ESA) in 1973.

The Endangered Species Act was established to slow the rate of extinction by giving at-risk animals and plants special protection, and to restore them in a healthy state within an ecosystem. It mandates federal agencies to use the best scientific evidence to list all species in danger of extinction as either *endangered* or *threatened* for these reasons: (1) present or threatened habitat degradation; (2) overutilization for commercial, recreational, scientific, or educational purposes; (3) disease or predation; (4) inadequacy of government regulatory mechanisms; (5) other natural or man-made factors affecting its continued existence. The act requires a recovery plan for "delisting" the species. In the quarter-century after enactment of the Endangered Species Act, the government has placed well over one thousand plants and animals under the law's protection. Two recent, notable successes of the ESA are America's once endangered national bird, the bald eagle, that was down listed from *endangered* to *threatened* status in 1995, and the peregrine falcon that was delisted in 1998.

California passed its own Endangered Species Act in 1984, thereby joining the federal government in establishing programs devoted to endangered species. By 1998, California had lost forty-six species, and had more endangered species (226), plus double the number of proposed species for designation than any other state. Of the twenty-one most endangered ecosystems identified by a U.S. Geological Survey, at least seven are in California, thus accounting for drastic declines in the state's biodiversity.

The endangered species acts are vitally important because laws protecting forests and watersheds, i.e. fish habitat, are either nonexistent, ineffective, or not being enforced. The Endangered Species Act extends its protections to these resources because they are critical to the survival of the species in question. For example, the spotted owl and the coho salmon are now protected by law whereas the old growth forests and rivers in which they respectively live may not have been. Now they too must be protected. Since habitat is crucial, environmentalists see the limitations of focusing on individual species instead of on broad ecosystems. But until something more protective comes along, the ESA is the best thing going to protect our native flora and fauna. However, the listing of a species is generally viewed as a last resort to prevent its extinction.

The specific categories for designating species under this legislation are:

Endangered Species (federal and state designations): A species in present danger of extinction throughout all or a significant part of its range.

Threatened Species (federal and state designations): A species likely to become endangered in the near future.

Species of Special Concern (a state designation): A species requiring special protection or management to prevent its ultimate extinction. This designation usually precedes the two formal listings above that place the species in a higher category of risk.

Watch List (federal and state designations): Declining species in need of periodic assessment (e.g. every five years), and included in a long-term protection plan.

Forest Ecosystem.

Species Protection vs. Resource Extraction

Persons sometimes question protecting an obscure plant or animal species, especially if protection jeopardizes economic gains. However, the vital interests of humans are inextricably linked to the preservation of biological species, be they plant or animal. In fact, few matters are more important to humankind.

Each species possesses unique genetic material evolved over thousands of years. Once destroyed, this one-of-a-kind source of information cannot be copied or retrieved. No matter how unimportant a species might seem, even an "inconsequential" snail darter, desert pupfish, or lowly fungus could be of incomparable value to humans. In fact, it was a "lowly fungus" from which man derived penicillin.

Each year, almost half of all prescriptions written in this country contain chemicals discovered in wild plants and animals, including penicillin, chloromycin, streptomycin, tetracycline, among others. Many diseases, e.g. bubonic plague, typhoid fever, diphtheria, scarlet fever, syphilis, bacterial pneumonia, have been successfully treated with medicines derived from wild plants. Extracts from a little known tropical flower, the rosy periwinkle, led to an effective drug for treating childhood leukemia.

Wild species also contain potential solutions to critical agricultural problems. The productivity of major crops cannot be sustained at present levels, or increased, unless there are new genetic breakthroughs, most of which will come from wild plants. The eating habits of a species may eliminate or control pests. Wild plants and animals have also produced chemicals used in hundreds of industrial products—plastics, deodorants, detergents, paints, paper products, coolants, lubricating oils, and waxes, to name a few. Biological diversity produces healthy economies in contrast to one based on a single product such as timber.

One symbolic target of critics of the Endangered Species Act has been the spotted owl. The issues here reveal how the demise of a single species has broad implications. As a raptor species, an owl (and eagles, hawks, falcons, ospreys, vultures) occupies the same position in the food chain as humans. If a raptor species declines, as the peregrine falcon did in the 1960s, we can assume there are underlying problems also threatening humans, such as the presence of chemicals and pesticides in the environment. And indeed it was the peregrine falcon's decline that exposed the persistent presence of DDT throughout the environment, posing a deadly threat to humans as well.

The health of varied bird species signal habitat changes potentially harmful to humans, e.g. the canary in the cave. What has been often lost in the spotted owl controversies is this broader issue of habitat, for any species is capable of surviving only if its habitat survives. The decline of the spotted owl indicates that its habitat—old growth forests—is also declining, a development posing dire consequences to humankind. Why is this so? Old growth forests give and preserve life by creating soil, preventing erosion, producing oxygen, and removing carbon dioxide and various pollutants from the atmosphere. Their rich soils produce nutrients critical for sustaining diverse plant life. Many bird and mammal species exist *only* in old growth forests whose very diversity and complexity ensure their survival. In contrast, the tree farms often replacing old growth forests after the latter are logged are simple monocultures incapable of sustaining biological diversity and capable of collapsing altogether, as for example from drought, fire, or insect infestations. Despite their crucial importance for sustaining life, *ninety percent of old growth forests have been eliminated in this country through logging.*

Just as the spotted owl serves as an indicator species for the health of old growth forests, fish species such as steelhead, coho salmon, and native trout dependent upon clean, cold waterways for survival are excellent indicator species for the health of our waterways. With fish, the issues are broader than mainly habitat as it is for the spotted owl. For example, to take more fish home to eat, many anglers wish to have plants of hatchery trout increased for wider stretches of river, with fewer restrictions on angling methods. However, such practices could threaten native and wild fish species—the most precious ones in any waterway. Wild fish possess unique physiological and biological traits specifically adapted to their environment as a result of natural selection, i.e. survival of the fittest. Among other things, they are more resistant to disease than introduced fish. When hatchery-reared trout are introduced to a river, these fish, bred in crowded and unnatural conditions, will often exhibit chaotic and aggressive behavior, disrupting the natural behavior patterns and territories of wild trout. Worse, hatchery trout can interbreed with wild trout, weakening the latter's genetic makeup, leading to the loss of genetic diversity within fish species and creating homogenized fish populations less equipped to survive.

A major issue in salmon (and steelhead) management has been a reliance on hatchery stock to restore fish populations, and the depletion of genetically pure wild fish populations. Wild salmon possess a genetic composition developed over centuries, providing them with unique qualities for their continuing life struggles. In contrast, possible evidence suggests that hatchery-reared fish comprise a genetically impure strain of salmon. Hatchery salmon are spawned in enclosures with other salmon, producing genetic interbreeding and possible genetic weakness. On their own they are less able to capture food due to their being fed in their early lives; they possess more of a pack tendency and increased aggression; they are more susceptible to diseases. The more hatchery fish come to dominate salmon populations, the more at risk wild salmon become.

It has only been in the last decades that fish biologists have been able to report that hatchery fish are often weaker specimens, capable of destroying through hybridization a native fish species. A healthy fishery depends not only on maintaining the genetic purity of a species, but also on the *diversity within subspecies of fish families*. For example, some location-specific populations of native fish, e.g. Pyramid Lake Lahontan cutthroat, grew to large sizes. Other strains of fish from different locations do not grow as large. The trait of largeness, as well as other distinc-tive traits, may belong to only one strain of the species, and once that population is eliminated, the trait may be lost forever.

Despite the threats of hatchery fish to wild and native fish populations, hatcheries and fish plants are fulfilling important and changing functions. Their historic purpose has been to raise fish for planting in waters with few or no fish, thus serving the recreational needs of anglers. The large majority of trout fishermen in California today fish for planted fish. Indeed, many popular fishing spots, such as the numerous lakes on the eastern Sierra Nevada, e.g. in Mammoth Lakes Basin and the June Lake Loop, are based almost exclusively on weekly hatchery plants. So too are heavily used urban fisheries. Many alpine lakes, including those holding golden trout, would be barren of fish were it not for plantings. (This practice has had detrimental effects on native alpine amphibians, in particular the mountain yellow-legged frog.)

A growing role of hatcheries is the rearing of native species whose very existence would be threatened were it not for these sanctuaries. In some cases, the recreational and preservation functions are combined as with Eagle Lake rainbows, a fishery maintained at present strictly through hatchery plants. Hatcheries are used to restock damaged waters, or waters chem-

Silver Lake in the June Lake Loop on the eastern Sierra Nevada, site for the state brook trout record in 1932, provides good lake fishing for planted rainbow trout. Photo by Mike Acker.

ically treated to eliminate an unwanted species. Hatcheries also allow for educational activities whereby youngsters and adults learn about fish. Fish biologists can study fish under controlled conditions in a hatchery thereby having them serve a critical research function.

Even though the roles of hatcheries have been evolving to reflect the changing priorities in fishery management, their costs are being questioned. The DFG spends three dollars on hatcheries for every dollar spent on habitat protection. Of the hatchery budget, one third is spent on trucking costs. Fish conservation groups are scrutinizing the millions of dollars spent each year to plant catchable trout (the most numerous hatchery-reared fish), especially considering their high mortality rate before anglers even catch them. Given the importance of native and wild fish populations over hatchery fish, more DFG monies might be allocated to fish habitat issues, and alternate ways investigated for fulfilling hatchery functions.

Habitat Issues. Any species is capable of surviving in its natural state only if its habitat is intact. For freshwater fish, habitat means life-sustaining water: rivers, streams, creeks, lakes, and ponds. The incomparable steelhead, if allowed, will use the complete waterway—from estuaries to headwaters. The lifelines for California's native species once were the state's magnificent array of rivers. Most have been thoroughly degraded.

A 1993 report sponsored by the State Lands Commission of California, entitled *California Rivers: A Public Trust Report,* concluded that the health of California's rivers are stressed and their viability as sustainable ecosystems in peril. It further stated, "it should no longer be disputed that there exists an urgent need for state agencies to undertake a comprehensive program of river basin and watershed protection and restoration."

What caused the deterioration in California's rivers? Many factors contributed. Mining certainly played an early role as environmentally disruptive methods to uncover gold and other minerals did untold damage to waterways. (Huge mounds of rock tailings still exist along some streams.) However, it was the post-depression economic boom in the state that led to massive environmental changes. By the 1940s, Shasta Dam on the Sacramento River and Friant Dam on the San Joaquin River, both constructed as part of the CVP, eliminated much of the historic salmon and steelhead spawning grounds upstream. Diversions, channelization, and the replace-

RIVER ECOSYSTEM

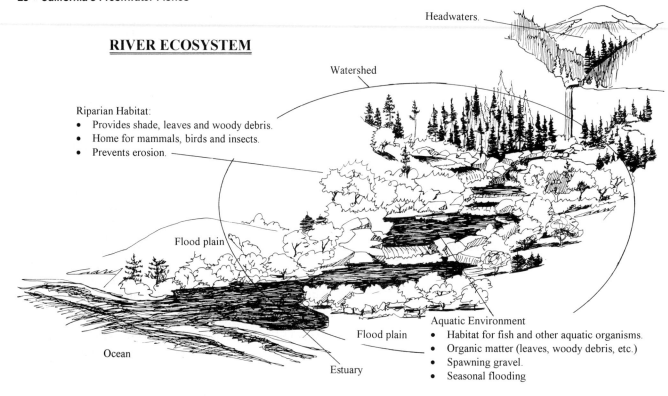

Headwaters.

Watershed

Riparian Habitat:
- Provides shade, leaves and woody debris.
- Home for mammals, birds and insects.
- Prevents erosion.

Flood plain

Ocean

Estuary

Flood plain

Aquatic Environment
- Habitat for fish and other aquatic organisms.
- Organic matter (leaves, woody debris, etc.)
- Spawning gravel.
- Seasonal flooding

River Ecosystem.

ment of riparian (riverside) growth with concrete and stone riprap degraded downstream habitat.

The full range of the Sierra Nevada has experienced severe deterioration of its aquatic and riparian habitats. Of sixty-seven types of aquatic habitat categorized for the Sierra Nevada, almost two-thirds are declining in quality and abundance, and many are at risk of disappearing altogether. The factors are many and cumulative, including: introductions of alien fishes, dams and diversions, alterations of stream channels, and watershed disturbances from grazing, mining, roads, and logging. According to the Sierra Nevada Ecosystem Project, grazing has been the largest cause of fish habitat degradation across the Sierra Nevada. For instance, in the South Fork Kern River, home of the Volcano Creek golden trout, excessive cattle grazing throughout this century has caused stream channel erosion, downcutting and lowering of the water table, river destabilization, and fecal contamination in various areas. The loss of riparian vegetation produces increased erosion and low water conditions, bringing too much heat in summer and too much ice in winter, effectively crippling the fishery.

The decline of chinook salmon points to another glaring case of habitat loss. In the nineteenth century, more than a million salmon spawned annually in the streams of the Sierra Nevada's west slope (e.g. Mokelumne, San Joaquin, Feather, Yuba, Tuolumne, Stanislaus, American, Merced, Kern, Kings), with some fish ascending up to 6,000 feet in elevation. The construction of multiple dams on these rivers blocked access to about ninety percent of the salmon's original spawning habitat. Consequently, chinook salmon have been virtually eliminated from the Sierra Nevada except for those still spawning in a few of the undammed tributaries to the Sacramento River, such as Deer Creek and Mill Creek.

Another dismal scene exists in the North Coast/Klamath region, heretofore renowned for its salmon and steelhead runs once extending up the Klamath River system all the way to Oregon. The construction of the Iron Gate Dam (1917-1922) on the Klamath near the Oregon border, along with other dams and diversions on rivers in the system, blocked fish migrations, reduced flows and increased water temperatures. Further, throughout this century the lumber industry crisscrossed the region with dirt roads while intensively harvesting the timber on inland watersheds, making them vulnerable to erosion, especially during the frequent heavy rainfall years common to the North Coast. By the 1960s, logjams and sediment clogged most of the area's salmon and steelhead habitat. Pesticide and fertilizer residues

Cattle along the South Fork Kern River in Templeton Meadows in the Golden Trout Wilderness. DFG photo by Christy McGuire .

from agricultural runoff further degraded the water quality. All of these factors contributed to an eighty percent (or higher) decline in salmon and steelhead numbers on the Klamath since the 1950s.

The construction of a dam in 1963 on a major tributary to the Klamath, the Trinity, blocked salmon and steelhead from their historic spawning areas there, and transferred ninety percent of the Trinity basin's water to southern California via the Sacramento River. The anadromous fishery in the Trinity declined by ninety percent soon thereafter.

As bad as the degradation of northern California's waterways has been, the picture only gets bleaker southward. In the eastern Sierra Nevada, numerous streams in the Mono Basin, including Lee Vining, Rush, Walker, and Parker creeks, historically emptied into Mono Lake. To the south, the extensive Owens River and its many tributaries flowed into Owens Lake, which once covered more than one hundred square miles and carried steamships hauling timbers and ore for the mining operations at Cerro Gordo. These waterways and the lower sections of scores of others provided some of the best brown trout fishing in the country, albeit due to initial introductions of trout at the end of the nineteenth and beginning of the twentieth centuries. However, the Los Angeles Department of Water and Power (LADWP) had earlier set the stage for one of the most notorious water diversions (many would call it a "steal") in this country.

Shortly after the turn of the twentieth century, the city of Los Angeles began aggressively buying a series of ranch lands holding water rights throughout the Owens Valley and Mono Basin. Once accomplished, by 1914 Los Angeles had completed the Owens Valley/Los Angeles Aqueduct that ultimately carried water from the Owens River southward to the San Fernando Valley. This project dried up ten miles of the lower Owens Gorge (which formerly held huge brown trout), many miles of the Owens River above Owens Lake, and Owens Lake itself, leaving in its place a basin of alkaline dust.

In addition, LADWP somehow secured from the state in the 1930s a license to export water from the Mono Basin. In 1941 it began diverting water from streams feeding Mono Lake to the upper Owens River through the Mono Craters Tunnel. A second aqueduct completed in the early 1970s diverted the remaining flows from Mono Lake's tributaries with the exception of the smaller Mill Creek. By 1982, with the lower sections of the tributaries now dry, the volume of the lake had dropped by half, threatening to destroy the lake's ecology. In the meantime, eastern Sierra Nevada water was allowing semi-arid Los Angeles to develop into the largest megalopolis in the world in terms of its sprawling geographic size.

Fortunately, legal actions, spurred by public outcries and the legal maneuvering of conservation groups (notably the Mono Lake Committee, Audubon Society, and California Trout), halted the diversions. Court decisions, applying the Public Trust Doctrine and a little known state statute requiring fish below a dam to be "maintained in good condition," mandate that the streams in Mono Basin must again flow with the necessary quantities of water to support fish and raise Mono Lake (which is too salty to support fish) back to its level before the diversions started. Further, the lower Owens Gorge, which had been dewatered since 1953, currently is receiving flows, the result of a penstock (a water pipe) breaking in 1991 allowing water to reenter the gorge, and subsequent pressure on LADWP to keep the water flowing. Rather than face another lawsuit, LADWP acquiesced. A robust brown trout fishery is quickly developing once again. Los Angeles has also been directed by the California Air Resources Board to solve the problems of dust from the dry Owens Lake. To its credit, LADWP has been enhancing recreational uses of their eastern Sierra Nevada lands and waters for the continuing enjoyment of a growing public, while contributing resources to the restoration and maintenance of fish habitat.

As mentioned above, the trout fishery in Mono Basin and Owens River drainage had been artificially created by the planting of non-native trout, especially the brown trout. The Owens River system historically contained only four native fishes: the Owens dace, sucker, chub, and pupfish. Part of the Owens Valley Aqueduct Project created reservoirs, principally Crowley Lake, Grant Lake, and Pleasant Valley Reservoir, that today offer outstanding trout fishing for both wild and planted rainbows and browns. Crowley also contains an abundance of Sacramento perch (illegally introduced in the 1960s), providing anglers with numerous catches and tasty fare. The outstanding fishing in the region today is a good example of how man's efforts at redistributing fish produced beneficial results for anglers, but exerted detrimental effects on native species. As a result of the major habitat changes, combined with the impact of the more predacious, competitive non-native game fishes, the Owens pupfish and chub are listed as *endangered* species, and the Owens dace is considered *threatened*.

Beyond the Owens Valley, southeastern California consists mainly of desert, including Death Valley

Crowley Lake offers outstanding angling for trout and Sacramento perch. Photo by Bob Madgic.

where the average rainfall is less than two inches. Here a phenomenal native fish has evolved—the pupfish—capable of surviving under the harshest of environmental conditions. It and other native fish of the Great Basin are endangered primarily from surface diversions and the pumping of underground aquifers that supply the necessary water to sustain these fish. The small quantities of available spring water are being transported to irrigate crops and fuel urban growth in the Southwest, including Las Vegas, threatening the very survival of the desert ecosystem and its native creatures.

The Colorado River system provides yet another stark example of severe habitat alteration. The Colorado flows from the Rocky Mountains to the Sea of Cortez in Mexico (Gulf of California), including 200 miles along the southeastern border of California. Historically, it was a very muddy and warm river, including its long run through the Grand Canyon. The lower Colorado, formerly deep and sluggish, consisted of a rich and diverse ecosystem encompassing river channels, sloughs and small back channels, marshes, willow scrub lands, cottonwood forests, and flood plain. Unique fish (and bird) species evolved in this river system, including the largest "minnow" in North America, the Colorado squawfish, capable of growing up to six feet in length and a hundred pounds in weight, and the razorback sucker, once the most abundant fish in the river and a staple food source for Native Americans.

A series of dams, including Glen Canyon and Hoover dams, created massive reservoirs, e.g. Lake Powell, Lake Mead, connected by channels of cold, clear water, dramatically changing the river and its fish. Introduced rainbow trout replaced native warm-water species in these stretches. Downstream from Lake Mead, the river warms and striped bass, channel and flathead catfish, largemouth bass, and other sunfish, occupy the waters. The lower Colorado has been thoroughly reconstructed by levees, smaller dams and impoundments, dredging, channelization, and bank stabilization using riprap. Essentially all of the river's flow is appropriated for consumption, divided among seven states and Mexico, with California taking by far the largest share. So much of the river's water is diverted that in some years none reaches the Gulf of California. The formerly extensive riparian habitat of this entire system is a small fraction of what it once was, and the many species unique to it are at critical risk of extinction.

The Los Angeles Basin also supported a rich fishery at one time. Today virtually all of the waterways in lowland areas once used by native fish, such as the

Santa Ana sucker, have been channelized, lined with concrete, and dewatered. In upland areas, most streams either have been dammed and diverted, or continually subjected to mass erosion of destabilized hillsides from road building, off-road vehicle use, gravel extraction, mining activities, grazing, and development of riparian areas.

Steelhead stocks that had adapted to the warmer waters of the region used to migrate up the coastal rivers, including some below California. However, dams, land development, and degradation of estuaries have so reduced water quantities that spawning and rearing habitat is virtually absent. So too are the former steelhead runs in any waterways south of Malibu Creek.

Notwithstanding the tremendous loss of natural habitat in southern California where sprawling urban growth reigns, many waters in the area hold a full array of inland fish species. Warmwater game species, including trophy-sized black bass, as well as trout species, occupy the numerous reservoirs. And wild trout exist in small mountain streams such as Deep Creek and Bear Creek in San Bernardino National Forest, and the West Fork of the San Gabriel in Angeles National Forest. These waters offer angling experiences in wilderness settings belying their proximity to Los Angeles.

While many of California's waterways have been degraded over decades, a river's deterioration can also be immediate and catastrophic. Two recent examples are the East Walker River in September 1988, and the Upper Sacramento River in July 1991—two of California's blue ribbon trout rivers. The East Walker's demise was caused by the draining of Bridgeport Reservoir by the Walker River Irrigation District of Nevada (WRID), which long controlled the water releases. The District, anticipating a shortage of water in the face of drought conditions, attempted to use California's water to fill its own reservoir far downstream in Nevada. In the process, silt from the drained Bridgeport Reservoir flushed down the channel and choked off the oxygen supply of thousands of fish. (A court later determined WRID did not possess autonomy over water releases from Bridgeport Reservoir, and adequate flows have to be maintained to protect the fishery. The river has successfully come back as a rich fishery.)

The story of the Upper Sacramento has been well told. On a July day in 1991, a railroad car turned over on a curve, dumping into the river a deadly chemical—metam sodium. The current carried the chemical downriver, killing every living organism in the forty-mile stretch from Dunsmuir to Lake Shasta. The river's complete rehabilitation, including the restoration of foliage and food chains to support the wild trout population, has been a lengthy process.

In the space of three years, two of California's richest wild trout rivers were ruined. The abrupt circumstances producing these catastrophes should alert us to the fragile nature of our waterways.

Following is a summary of the most harmful threats to rivers and river habitats:

Grazing. The American Fishery Society has identified grazing as the primary cause of fishery degradation in the West. Over grazing eradicates native plant species, and destroys delicate riverine systems. Cattle chisel and trample stream banks, widening channels, increasing erosion, warming waters and contaminating them with fecal matter. Grazing has permanently damaged many Sierra Nevada meadows and streams.

Dams and Diversions. Dams starve rivers of oxygen and cause highly fluctuating temperatures and flows—all destructive to plant life and fisheries. Dams trap gravel, sediment, and food that otherwise flow downstream. They block the movement of migratory and anadromous fish such as salmon, steelhead, and sea-run trout. Diversions (e.g. aqueducts, irriga-

Bear Creek in San Bernadino National Forest. DFG photo by Ray Ally.

tion channels, recreational uses) rob streams and rivers of their full supply of water, often with disastrous ecological results.

Agriculture. Farming practices are the primary source of pollutants (e.g. sediment, animal waste, nutrients, pesticides) in waterways. Toxic substances in herbicides and pesticides absorbed on soil particles enter streams from soil leaching. Agriculture alters river-riparian ecosystems.

Flood Control and Channelization. Channelization causes the loss of habitat diversity created by bends, pool/riffle sequences, sunken woody debris, and other irregularities. It destroys riparian habitat and eliminates the shading and food production provided by overhanging vegetation to the detriment of the aquatic community.

Exhaust and Chemical Emissions. Pollutants from farm chemicals and exhaust emissions, both auto and industrial, produce smog carried to the Sierra Nevada, harming flora and fauna. Acidification occurs when nitrous oxides and sulfur dioxides from emissions are transformed into nitric and sulfuric acids, forming acid rain and snow that damage trees, water quality, and fisheries.

Mining. Aggregate mining, the largest mining industry in California, alters stream beds and destroys river habitats. Toxic substances from mines spill into streams and rivers. Pollutants are leached from the ores into the waterways. Suction-dredge gold mining "vacuums" the bottoms of rivers with destructive results to their ecology.

Timber Harvest. Timber production and logging roads alter watersheds by increasing runoff and delivery of fine sediment to stream channels, decreasing summer flows, increasing upland erosion and altering natural drainage patterns. As a result, riparian habitat is damaged or destroyed, adversely affecting water quality and increasing its temperature.

Urbanization. Urbanization places structures in the path of natural processes. Deposits from the urbanscape, including trace metals such as cadmium, copper, lead and zinc, vehicular gasoline, and oil residues, find their way into waterways through runoff and drainage systems.

Recreation. Trash and litter pollute river environments. Sewage from marinas is often disposed of directly into the rivers, an illegal action not effectively monitored. Through human carelessness, fueling accidents, leaky tanks and lines, allow spilled oil, diesel, gasoline, paint and toxic chemicals to enter rivers. Two-stroke engines on motor boats and personal watercrafts discharge quantities of contaminants into the water.

Riverside Development. Development destroys riparian habitat. Flood control measures result in further vegetation removal. Today, even with at least eighty to ninety percent of riparian habitat in most western states eliminated, the remaining pieces are still being threatened by development. Development in flood plains creates a need for dams and levees that destroy fish and wildlife habitat while placing more people and property at risk.

Responsible Stewardship. Responsible stewardship today requires passing on a natural world more restored, more intact, than what has been given to us. To the degree possible, California's native fish in their pure genetic makeup should be rendered healthy once again and fish habitat restored. It is not enough to simply maintain what we presently have.

The issues involved in supporting fish populations and their habitat are complex. With California's population expected to double over the next century, and the ongoing development of land, human demands for the life sustenance of fish—water—will surely increase. The balancing of human needs with those of nature's other creatures poses daunting challenges. The following guidelines, representing a summary of the foregoing pages, are presented as an agenda for responsible stewardship:

Commitment to the Wisdom of Nature and Natural Processes. In the past, America viewed its mission primarily as one of "conquering" nature and native creatures, including native peoples. Americans literally attempted to eradicate all predator species, including wolves, grizzly bears, eagles, hawks, mountain lions, rattlesnakes, and bobcats. By upsetting natural balances, many of man's manipulations of nature have produced unforseen and damaging consequences. While philosophers and naturalists have long preached of nature's wisdom, it's only in recent decades that scientists have affirmed that the process of natural selection, the basis for evolution, should be left to function without interference when and where possible.

Commitment to Preserving Native Creatures. California's native fish still existing in their pure genetic makeup must be saved, preserved, restored, and nurtured. Preserving some native species such as the Kern River rainbow or the Lahontan cutthroat by restoring them back in their native waters must often be accompanied by eradicating from these waters other introduced species such as rainbow and brown trout. Destructive and threatening alien species, e.g.

the northern pike, should be eliminated where this is feasible. Economic and other costs accompany these procedures. For instance, anglers may resist the elimination of brown trout from their fishing waters in favor of the restoration of Lahontan cutthroat. This stance, however, undermines the greater value due native creatures.

Wild Fish Preferred Over Hatchery Specimens. Game fish able to adapt and propagate within their aquatic settings are the more valued creatures, except in places where they threaten native fish. The fostering of wild fish populations is critical to a healthy fishery, and far less costly in economic terms than one dependent on hatchery programs.

Protection, Restoration, and Preservation of Habitat. Habitat means wildlife; eliminate the habitat and you eliminate wildlife. For fish, healthy aquatic ecosystems represent the necessary habitat. Given the costly measures required to repair damaged habitat, healthy habitat must be protected first and foremost.

Adoption of Land Ethic. Famed conservationist, Aldo Leopold, in his classic 1949 publication, *A Sand County Almanac*, issued a prescient call for humans to be respectful citizens of the land-community rather than be the conqueror of it. In this enlightened role, humans would co-exist with other creatures in a har-

Small creek on eastern Sierra Nevada holding pure Lahontan cutthroat trout. Note the effort to stabilize the creek's bank, which was degraded from grazing and logging practices. Photo by Bob Madgic.

monious relationship. Knowing what we know today on how humankind's future well-being is interconnected with biological diversity, it is critical for humans and nations to adopt policies and pursue actions that protect our fellow creatures.

Implications. The priorities of responsible stewardship are not easily carried out. Diverse human interests often clash; many do not place a high value on native and wild fish species. However, responsible stewardship requires individuals to rise above narrow and selfish interests. Anglers and commercial fishermen, farmers and ranchers who want to see their lands maintained as open space rather than developed, conservationists and lovers of nature, outdoor recreationists including boaters, hunters, bird watchers, and hikers—all should share a common interest in preserving wildlife habitat. Polls show that a large majority of Americans (and Californians) support environmental preservation. This national priority must be embedded within the nation's culture and translated into specific custodial measures for wild creatures.

Government agencies have not always provided responsible stewardship for our native lands and creatures. Government agencies constructed huge dams, eliminated native creatures, introduced alien fish species that wreaked havoc on native fish, and gave priority to grazing, logging and mining on public lands. Nonetheless, government agencies today, acting in behalf of the public trust, are primarily responsible for providing stewardship for our lands and wildlife. In our democracy, government is most responsive when the will of the people is clear. With many governmental decisions, votes count more than good science. Thus the impetus for responsible stewardship comes first and foremost from involved and vocal citizens who support stewardship priorities.

Consider the efforts to restore native trout to their ancestral waters. To achieve this objective, government officials may first have to eliminate other trout species from these waters by chemically treating the water. Using chemicals, e.g. rotenone, has been shown to be effective without harm either to people or to the environment. Rotenone is a natural substance derived from several tropical and sub-tropical plants, and used by native peoples in Central and South America to kill fish for their consumption. Farmers today can use rotenone and still have their produce certified as "organic." Rotenone is so safe to humans that it is exempt from tolerance on fruits and vegetables.

There are individuals and groups who will ignore, resist, or even subvert government efforts to preserve and protect native creatures. Poaching and outright acts of sabotage, e.g. illegal replantings of fish in waters the DFG chemically treated to eliminate such species, regularly happen. It is important for citizens to influence and support government in the protection of public resources.

Economic considerations drive public decisions probably more than any other factor. Studies are showing that environmental preservation and related recreation, tourism, and service-oriented industries are producing economic growth in communities formerly wedded to older industries such as logging and mining. Recreational fishing is the most popular of all sports in numbers of participants, and it continues to grow in popularity. According to a University of California 1995 report, sportfishing employs 153,000 Californians and provides five billion dollars annually to the state's economy, or one dollar for every hundred dollars spent in the state.

Lastly, those persons whose avocations and livelihoods are intertwined with fish, e.g. anglers, fishing guides, resort owners, commercial fishermen, have the greatest responsibility to be good stewards for these creatures and the places where they live. To pursue short-sighted and selfish actions that deplete these finite resources is self-defeating and contrary to one's obligation to the community at large. As one example, anglers sometimes join those opposed to listing a fish species as *threatened* or *endangered* because of the restrictions on fishing that follow. But if a fish population crashes in the absence of protections, then everybody loses.

Indicators of Progress. Fortunately, progress is being made across a number of fronts with stewardship priorities. Consider:

★ The courts have been applying the Public Trust Doctrine, a doctrine going back to the Roman Empire and containing the idea that certain common properties such as rivers, the seashore, and the air are held by the government in trusteeship for the free and unimpeded use of the general public. In a series of cases, the courts have decided: trout are public property and subject to the Public Trust Doctrine; streams must be rewatered and fisheries restored to conditions in existence before water diversions degraded them; fish below dams must be kept in "good condition."

★ Some dams are being torn down, opening up spawning areas for salmon and steelhead once again.

★ Today thirty-five of the finest trout waters in California are managed within a wild trout program by the DFG, designed to foster a self-sustaining wild trout population in each.

Fly fishing on the Upper Owens River. Photo by Bob Madgic.

★ "Catch-and-Release" angling is required in nearly 1000 miles of streams and in six lakes; many anglers now carry out this practice on their own.

★ Many previously dry waterways have been rewatered, including sections of the Lower Owens, Rush Creek, Lee Vining Creek, the Pit River below Lake Britton, Bear Creek below Big Bear Lake, and Alameda Creek (in progress).

★ Flow releases from dams and the rivers below them are being managed to improve downstream habitat through increased minimum flows and occasional flooding or flushing, and to foster fish populations.

★ New fishways are being established to provide access for anadromous fish where barriers existed.

★ Government agencies historically emphasizing resource extraction, e.g. the U.S. Forest Service, now are placing greater importance on resource management and preservation.

★ Programs to restrict grazing and logging are being implemented.

★ The State of California is instituting a Heritage Trout Program to restore and protect the state's native trout species and their original habitats.

★ The State has adopted a *California Steelhead Restoration and Management Plan.*

★ Progress is being made in restoring native fish, e.g. Lahontan cutthroat and the Little Kern golden trout.

★ State and federal agencies have joined to form the CALFED Bay-Delta Program that is dedicated to the development of a long-term solution to fish and wildlife, ecosystem restoration and preservation, water supply reliability, flood control, and water quality problems in the Bay-Delta Estuary. The majority of citizens who responded to CALFED's environmental draft urged conservation and water use efficiency, rather than building more dams and reservoirs. (It remains to be seen how effective the CALFED Bay-Delta Program will be in meeting its conservation objectives.)

The Kern River in Sequoia National Forest. DFG photo by Dan Christensen, retired fisheries biologist.

Coldwater Game Fish: Salmonidae Family

Coldwater fish species in streams and rivers require: sufficient quantities and depth of clean water year round; high turbulence and oxygen content with proper current velocity; gravel, stone beds, and adequate space for spawning and the growth of eggs, young, and juveniles; adequate food supplies; and a temperature range seldom exceeding 68° F. In lakes, coldwater species need (in addition to the above elements except for those specific to moving water) adequate quantities of cold water, which generally means the lower strata of a large, deep lake during the hot months. To allow propagation, the lakes must have a feeder stream for fish to spawn, except in the case of brook trout that are sometimes able to spawn in lakes without one by utilizing gravel beds and springs. In alpine settings, a lake must not freeze totally over.

Anadromous species—salmon, steelhead, coastal cutthroat trout—require unimpeded migratory passages to their natural spawning areas with free access to the ocean and back. While other species utilize sections of rivers, steelhead, if not blocked by impassable constructions, will often migrate from the ocean clear up to the headwaters of rivers and streams. Thus, all elements in the waterway must be in good condition for steelhead to thrive.

Migrating salmon. Six Rivers National Forest photo.

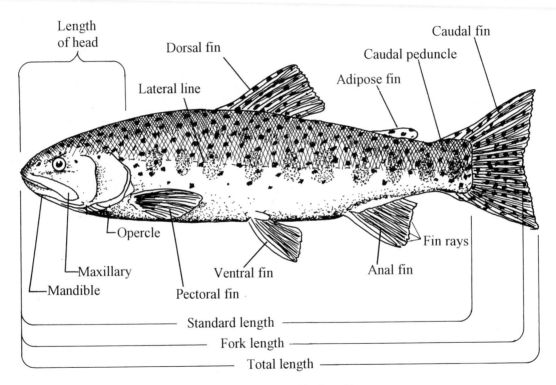

External Anatomy of Salmonid.

Lower Bull Frog Lake at the headwaters of the Little Kern River. DFG photo by Christy McGuire.

Golden Trout

California is the only state where the golden trout is native. Its original distribution was restricted to the Kern River drainage in Tulare County. However, golden trout have since been planted in other regions of California and the West. Goldens will interbreed with rainbow trout if they occupy the same water, thus producing a hybridized creature often more like a rainbow than a golden. To protect the purity of the native golden trout, it is crucial that its habitat be free from rainbow and other trout species.

Golden trout are valued as much or more for their beauty and scarcity than their sporting and Epicurean qualities. It usually takes some effort to get to the alpine waters holding these beautiful creatures. When found in mountain streams—their natural environment—they typically are less than ten inches and usually easy to catch. In high elevation lakes where they have been planted, primarily from 8,000 to 10,500 feet, goldens in the twelve-to-eighteen-inch range can be found, and usually are not easy to catch.

The state record stands at nine pounds, eight ounces, taken from Virginia Lake in Fresno County in 1952.

Volcano Creek Golden (California Golden Trout)
Oncorhynchus mykiss aquabonita
(Native; special concern)

The Volcano Creek golden, California's state fish, is considered one of the most beautiful fish in the world. It is distinguished primarily by its bright gold flanks, a red-orange lateral band, and olive parr marks.

Native to Golden Trout Creek and a tributary, Volcano Creek, and in the South Fork of the Kern River and most of its tributaries, the Volcano Creek golden, also called the California golden trout, has been planted throughout California's waters, primarily in alpine lakes. In many of these, periodic restocking must take place or else the goldens disappear due to lack of spawning streams. Although now distributed widely, its original environment has been degraded primarily as a result of cattle grazing still permitted in the designated Golden Trout Wilderness, created in 1977 by the U.S. Congress to protect the golden's historical habitat. Another threat is contamination through interbreeding with rainbow trout, and from competition and eventual domination (to the point of elimination) from brown trout in waters they co-inhabit.

Volcano Creek Golden (California Golden Trout).

Little Kern Golden
Oncorhynchus mykiss whitei
(Native; federally threatened)

The Little Kern golden's native home is confined to the Little Kern River drainage. This subspecies doesn't possess the dominant golden hues of the Volcano Creek golden, resembling more a rainbow trout. It's a small fish, rarely exceeding twelve inches. It is usually profusely spotted, with a red band and olive parr marks on its sides. When the fish first emerges from the water, gold specks may be visible before quickly fading.

Rainbow trout, thoughtlessly introduced into the watershed mostly during the 1930s, interbred with the goldens and produced hybridized fish. By the early 1970s, the Little Kern golden had all but disappeared from ninety percent of its native habitat, then occupying only ten miles of stream. In 1975, the DFG launched an effort to restore this unique fish to all of its historic habitat by restocking pure Little Kern golden trout in sections where hybridized populations were previously eliminated by chemical treatments of the water. The DFG constructed artificial barriers to prevent other trout species from reentering the restored section of stream. These efforts have been initially successful as over eighty miles of stream, and headwater lakes, have been restored to the Little Kern golden trout, a project that requires ongoing monitoring.

Little Kern Golden Trout.

Cutthroat Trout

The cutthroat is one of the West's oldest natives, historically enjoying a wide distribution from the Rocky Mountains to the West Coast. Its name is derived from distinctive red-orange stripes or slashes on the underside of the lower jaw. As with other native fishes, its well-being has been sacrificed to the distribution of more aggressive trout species. The three native subspecies of cutthroat trout in California are Lahontan, Paiute, and coastal cutthroat. These are fragile trout still fighting to survive.

The state record for a cutthroat is a thirty-one pound, eight ounce Lahontan cutthroat, caught in Lake Tahoe in 1911.

Llewellyn Falls on Silver King Creek. DFG photo by Eric Gerstung.

Lahontan Cutthroat
Oncorhynchus clarki henshawi
(Native; federally threatened)

The Lahontan cutthroat, formerly called a "black-spotted trout," is characterized by red-orange slash marks under each jaw with a profusion of black spots over its body. Traces of a reddish streak are often visible along its sides.

In the past, the Lahontan cutthroat was one of the most sought-after fish in California due to its enormous size and tasty flesh. Lahontan cutthroats over twenty pounds were once common, rivaling the Pacific Coast salmon in size. The fish actually grew upwards of sixty pounds, making it the largest trout in North America. Its native range was a massive prehistoric lake, Lake Lahontan, that covered much of Nevada and parts of California. When it receded, Pyramid Lake and Walker Lake remained, holding abundant Lahontan populations, as did Lake Tahoe. The Truckee and Walker rivers, as well as some of their tributaries, provided the lake-dwelling fish in Pyramid and Walker lakes with their principal spawning grounds, with annual runs up the Truckee alone numbering in the tens of thousands.

During spawning runs from Pyramid, Walker, and Tahoe lakes at the end of the eighteenth century, market fishermen netted or trapped huge quantities of the fish in both the lakes and their tributaries. Subsequent damming of the Truckee and Walker rivers, in particular the Derby Dam on the Truckee River in 1905, and a series of dams on the Walker River, kept the Lahontan from reaching its historic spawning reaches. Although some Lahontans continued to spawn below the dams, by 1938 the water quality had become so thoroughly degraded as a result of diversions, reduced flows, and sawmill and pulp mill pollution, that the spawning ceased. As a result, the great Lahontan cutthroats were eliminated from Pyramid and Walker lakes. The Lahontan population formerly in Lake Tahoe was also extirpated during the 1930s, a result of overharvesting, habitat changes, and competition from introduced lake trout. Several attempts to restore this fishery with planted Lahontans were unsuccessful.

With the loss of the original strain of Lahontan, reestablishing a cutthroat trout sport fishery in Pyramid Lake has consisted of stocking a hatchery-reared fish. In contrast to Pyramid Lake, a remnant of the Walker Lake strain was saved and is being artificially propagated by the Nevada Fish and Game Department for stocking Walker Lake. However, the native stream-dwelling populations of cutthroat trout formerly within the Truckee, Carson, Walker, Quinn and Humboldt rivers have been largely displaced by introduced rainbow, brown, and brook trout.

Fortunately, some genetically pure Lahontan cutthroat remained in a few small, headwater tributaries. To establish self-sustaining populations over a broader geographical area, both California and Nevada fisheries personnel are continuing to transplant these pure Lahontan cutthroats to other ancestral streams where non-native trout have been chemically eradicated. Paiute Indians who own Pyramid Lake have also been propagating genetically pure Lahontans and repopulating the lake with them. However, it appears as though the particular strain of Lahontan that grew to large sizes may have been lost, demonstrating that diversity within a species is often critically important for preserving a unique trait held by select members of the species.

Despite efforts to restore the Lahontan fishery in Pyramid Lake, it remains at risk. Continued water diversions upstream of the lake threaten to deprive it of sufficient water to keep it from becoming too alkaline to sustain a fishery. Lahontan cutthroat trout are still unable to reproduce in the Truckee and Walker rivers because of obstructing dams, excessive diversions of water for irrigation, and pollution from agricultural runoff.

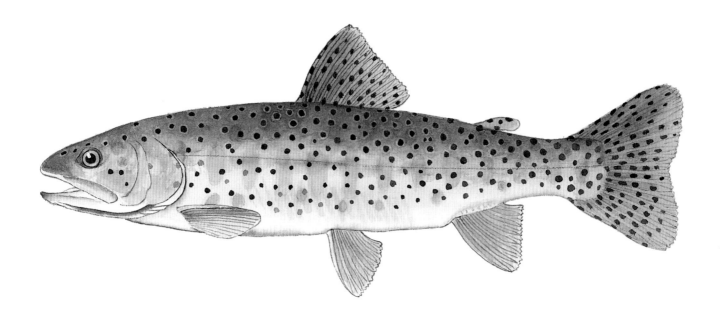

Lahontan Cutthroat Trout.

Paiute Cutthroat
Oncorhynchus clarki seleniris
(Native; federally threatened)

A strikingly beautiful fish, the Paiute cutthroat is the rarest of all California trout. It is native only to the Silver King Creek drainage, tributary to the East Carson River within the Carson-Iceberg Wilderness. The Paiute is a small trout, rarely exceeding fourteen inches in streams. Its color ranges from dusky rose to golden yellow with faint parr marks, scarlet lateral lines, and distinctive light orange slash marks. In contrast to other cutthroat subspecies, it is almost or totally spotless.

The Paiute's population, once numbering in the thousands, was contaminated by a 1949 unauthorized introduction of rainbow trout in Silver King Creek that hybridized with the Paiute. Fortunately, the DFG had previously transported a few fish in 1947 to a small tributary above a waterfall, safeguarding a small population of Paiute from interbreeding. Once the DFG recognized this fish's fragile existence, it eradicated the hybrid fish from Silver King Creek and restocked it with pure Paiute cutthroats captured above the previously noted waterfall.

Despite the DFG's restoration efforts, the Paiute's future is still not secure as a catastrophic event such as a drought or fire, or illegal fishing, could wipe out the small population of these rare creatures. Silver King Creek also has been damaged by cattle grazing and alien beaver that have decimated the aspen forests along the stream. Future efforts will be made to expand Paiutes to lower Silver King Creek. It is hoped that eventually a sport fishery will be established for the Paiute cutthroat, but first their numbers must increase and their population range become expanded.

Paiute Cutthroat Trout.

Coastal Cutthroat
Oncorhynchus clarki clarki
(Native; special concern)

Coastal cutthroat trout, ranging from southeastern Alaska down to the Eel River, are similar to steelhead rainbow trout in life history and appearance. However, the former has more spots, especially below the lateral line, generally lacking in steelhead. Because of its ties to the ocean, the coastal cutthroat may be the original cutthroat species from which the other cutthroat subspecies evolved.

Like salmon, coastal cutthroats return to the same waters to spawn. However, in contrast to both salmon and steelhead, it prefers the smaller coastal streams for spawning. Their numbers have surely declined over decades as a result of damage to these streams from logging and other human activities, and the dredging and filling of estuaries where coastal cutthroats spend considerable time.

Because they are difficult to distinguish from rainbow trout, exact numbers of coastal cutthroats are difficult to ascertain, but their numbers are not great. In California, their largest distribution (thirty percent) is in the Smith River drainage where fourteen- to eighteen-inch fish are common. Overall, anglers and fish managers have not given this anadromous fish much attention due to the greater importance placed on salmon and steelhead.

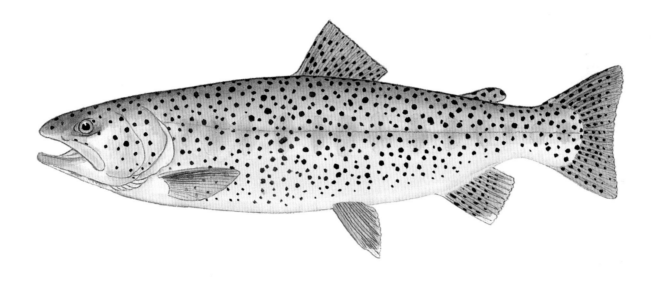

Coastal Cutthroat Trout.

Rainbow Trout

The rainbow trout is California's most abundant trout, occupying many of the state's cold streams and lakes. Its dominant visual characteristic from which the name "rainbow" is derived is the light red lateral band along its sides. Its origins go back to the anadromous coastal rainbow (steelhead). Resident subspecies, including the McCloud River redband and the Kern River rainbow, evolved above impassable waterfalls that kept them from interbreeding with the coastal rainbow. Another subspecies exists in Eagle Lake where it adapted to the highly alkaline waters of the lake. Except for these three inland subspecies, the distinctiveness of the varied rainbow populations has been largely diluted through widespread intermingling among the respective strains and the extensive plantings of hatchery-reared fish.

The average size of rainbow populations depends upon their homewaters, with some populations averaging a mere six to nine inches, and others averaging sixteen inches. Adult steelhead typically measure twenty to thirty inches in length, and five to fifteen pounds in weight. The state record for a rainbow (a steelhead) is twenty-seven pounds, four ounces from the Smith River, Del Norte County, 1976.

Common Rainbow
Oncorhynchus mykiss ssp.
(Native)

The rainbow trout is a California native whose progeny have been distributed throughout the country and world. The typical rainbow has a dark greenish to bluish topside, and black spots on its tail and back. Some rainbows are silvery in color with less conspicuous spotting. Others may be completely covered with spots. These wide variations in coloration are a result of: 1) distinctiveness of subspecies; 2) widespread mixing among the populations; 3) adaptations to local conditions. Varied genetic compositions of ancestral origins also produce behavioral differences among rainbow strains. For example, some rainbows in coastal waterways want to migrate to the ocean while others in the same river do not.

Hundreds of thousands of artificially propagated rainbows are produced each year in hatcheries and planted in the state's waters. They are typically more pale and wan in color due to constant exposure to sunlight in a hatchery, with rounded tailfins caused by crowded conditions in concrete channels. Their dorsal and adipose fins are usually shrunken and deformed from ultraviolet radiation.

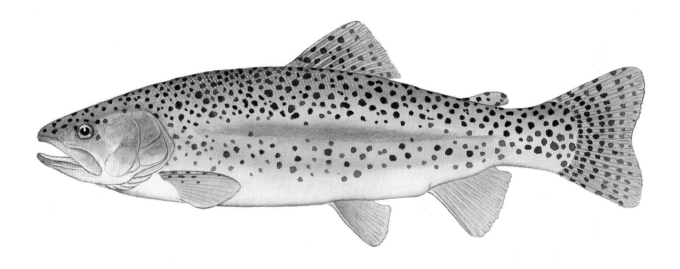

Rainbow Trout (McCloud River Strain).

Coastal Rainbow or Steelhead
Oncorhynchus mykiss irideus
(Native; central coast, south-central coast, and Central Valley steelhead are threatened; southern steelhead are endangered)

This legendary silvery fish, an anadromous rainbow trout called steelhead, has long been prized by anglers. Adult steelhead possess blue-green backs with dark spots, and silver sides grading to silver-white on their undersides. During the summer, some adults may have the pale red lateral stripes characteristic of rainbows. A steelhead rarely possesses any spots below the lateral line whereas most resident rainbows do. In California rivers most steelhead will be between twenty and twenty-five inches, and from five to ten pounds. However steelhead over thirty inches in length and in excess of fifteen pounds migrate up a few rivers. In particular, the Smith River holds large winter-run steelhead.

Of all major California salmonids, with the exception of coho salmon and Lahontan cutthroat, steelhead have suffered the most dramatic decline in distribution. They once thrived in the coastal rivers from Baja, California, to the Oregon border, and in the Sacramento and San Joaquin river systems. Today, good-sized runs remain only in the Russian,

Klamath River. Six Rivers National Forest photo.

Eel, Klamath, and Smith rivers. Overall, numbers of steelhead have declined from about 600,000 mostly wild adults in the early 1960s to about 200,000 to 250,000 mostly hatchery-reared adults today.

All hatchery steelhead have their adipose fin clipped to distinguish them from wild fish and to trace their movements. The dorsal fin of the hatchery fish is also usually eroded. To preserve and bolster the numbers of wild fish, anglers are required to release wild steelhead on all California streams except for the Smith River.

Steelhead have distinct life history groupings: summer steelhead, spring-run steelhead, winter northern steelhead, winter southern steelhead, and fall steelhead. The fall runs begin toward the end of the summer in the bigger rivers such as the Klamath. In the smaller coastal waterways where sandbars have formed at their mouths, the runs begin after the first rains wash out the sandbars. The most abundant is the winter run in the North Coast waterways, with the peak runs typically in January, February, and March. Spring runs (also called "summer steelhead"), while never abundant in California, have declined to a small fraction of their original numbers, with less than one hundred fish showing in the few rivers still with runs.

Angler on the Klamath River. Photo by Bob Madgic.

Smaller steelhead entering the Klamath system later in the summer and early fall are often referred to as "half pounders." These are immature fish that have spent only a few months in the ocean before their first upstream migration. If they survive, they will return to the ocean in the spring, and migrate back up the river as adults the following spring. Half pounders on average range in size from ten to eighteen inches in length, and from a half pound to three pounds in weight.

Like salmon, steelhead manifest an inherent drive to return to the waterway where they were spawned, i.e. their natal waters. However, more steelhead appear to stray to different waterways than salmon generally do, perhaps prompted by variations in water temperatures and cleanliness. (Research hasn't produced any definitive findings here.) Many other decided differences exist between the two species. For example, with the exception of the coho salmon, salmon fingerlings generally return to sea after only a few months in fresh water. Steelhead fingerlings stay in rivers for two years, thus requiring cold water, deep pools, and riparian habitat over that time. Unlike salmon, steelhead generally do not die after spawning and a small percentage of them may return from the ocean to spawn again.

Steelhead also use, if possible, almost all portions of a river's system—from estuaries to headwaters. Beyond any other species, even salmon, steelhead exhibit tremendous determination and strength in migrating up crashing rivers with steep drops.

To restore steelhead to their historic distribution range in the Central Valley, upstream access must be provided, as well as increased cold water releases below dams and diversions. For the North Coast, waterways require increased water flows from dams, e.g. Iron Gate Dam on the Klamath, Lewiston Dam on the Trinity, habitat restoration, and reductions in disturbances to water quality. Along the South Coast, barriers to migrations upstream have to be removed or modified, streamflows restored, spawning and rearing areas protected, and fish stocks reintroduced where they have disappeared.

In 1996 the DFG published *Steelhead Restoration and Management Plan for California,* the blueprint for the Department's efforts to restore this prized, and oftentimes overlooked, fish.

Coastal Rainbow Trout. (Steelhead).

Eagle Lake Rainbow
Oncorhynchus mykiss aquilarum
(Native; special concern)

The Eagle Lake rainbow evolved in the highly alkaline waters of its namesake lake, thus giving the fish a unique genetic structure. It is a brighter and more robust trout due to its rich environment. It also lives longer and grows larger than other rainbow subspecies, thus making it a good game fish.

At one time, Eagle Lake produced so many trout over five pounds that huge quantities were harvested for commercial purposes. Unfortunately, its primary spawning stream, Pine Creek, has suffered degradation from cattle grazing, logging, road building, and railroad track building. By 1960, the Eagle Lake rainbow was nearly extinct. The DFG artificially propagated fish to save the subspecies and restore a population to Eagle Lake, mainly for sport-fishing purposes. Today plantings of hatchery-reared fish maintain the fishery, which averages trout eighteen to twenty-two inches in length, and three to four pounds in weight. Eagle Lake rainbows are also planted in other waters in the state.

Eagle Lake has to be a healthy lake if the Eagle Lake rainbow is to survive as a distinct subspecies. If the lake loses too much water, increased alkalinity may kill off the trout. A plan is being developed to restore natural spawning to Pine Creek, which will require the removal of competing brook trout.

Eagle Lake Rainbow Trout.

Redband

Oncorhynchus mykiss ssp.

(Native; special concern and candidate for federally threatened status)

The origin and place of the redband trout within fish taxonomies is unclear, although they are considered a subspecies of rainbow trout. It is a strikingly beautiful trout with distinctive coloration, possessing a yellowish to orange body color with a brick-red lateral stripe and white-tipped bottom fins. The adults retain their parr marks. There are actually three distinct subspecies of redband trout: The McCloud River redband trout, the Goose Lake redband trout, and the Warner Valley redband trout.

The McCloud River redband trout is unique to the upper McCloud River and its tributaries. It is believed to have evolved above geological barriers, primarily the middle waterfall of the upper McCloud, that separated it from its anadromous ancestor—the coastal rainbow. Today it's found in tiny Sheepheaven Creek at the headwaters of the McCloud River and in other small tributaries (Trout, Swamp, Tate, Edson, and Moosehead creeks). It's a small fish, rarely exceeding seven inches.

Other lineages of redband trout are found in Goose Lake in northeastern California, and the Warner Valley in southeastern Oregon. These two redband subspecies are able to survive in much warmer waters than other rainbow trout. The Warner Valley redband historically migrated during wet climate cycles between mountain streams (some originate in California), where they spawned and reared, and basin lakes, where they grew large eating invertebrates and smaller fish. Their environments have been degraded from the blocking of spawning runs by irrigation dams, the removal of riparian growth on the streams from logging and grazing, and the introduction of carp, which muddies the waters in the lakes. Altogether the three subspecies of redband trout are now eliminated from over seventy percent of their native ranges.

McCloud River Redband Trout.

Kern River Rainbow
Oncorhynchus mykiss gilberti
(Native; special concern)

The Kern River rainbow occupies part of the Kern River watershed, and is generally believed to have descended from a mix of the coastal rainbow and the Little Kern golden, followed by isolation leading to its unique features. The Kern River rainbow typically possesses heavier spotting over most of its body than other rainbow subspecies. It is also capable of growing bigger than many of its cousins, up to twenty inches in the main stem of the Kern. When first lifted from the water, it appears to have a bluish cast to it.

Given the narrow range of this rare fish, its future is precarious. Habitat damage from natural causes such as floods, drought, or fire, from the alien beaver, and from the threat of interbreeding with other trout species, all can jeopardize the Kern River rainbow's future. Its uniqueness mandates attention and management decisions to ensure its survival. Special catch and release regulations have been established for portions of the upper Kern River.

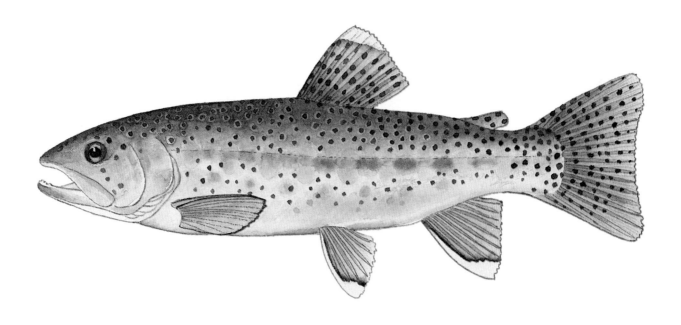

Kern River Rainbow Trout.

Mountain Whitefish
Prosopium williamsoni
(Native)

The mountain whitefish is an odd salmonid. In contrast to trout and salmon, whitefish lack strong teeth, possess a moderately inferior mouth, large scales, and short dorsal fins. It is a bottom feeder and often mistaken for a sucker. The main differences between the two species are: the mountain whitefish's mouth is not as low below its snout as is the sucker's; the whitefish possesses an adipose fin like other salmonids whereas sucker species do not; the coloration of mountain whitefish is more silvery on its sides and brownish on top. The mountain whitefish has limited distribution in California, being found only in the Truckee, Carson, and Walker river drainages where they are native. (It is more prevalent in other western states, particularly Montana.)

The state record is one pound, eight ounces, taken from the East Carson River in 1994.

Bull Trout
Salvelinus confluentus
(Native; extinct)

The bull trout formerly occurred in the McCloud River drainage below the Lower Falls. The bull trout is a char rather than a trout, but the similarities are so close that it and other chars are listed as "trout." It was California's only native char.

A close relative of the Dolly Varden trout, the bull trout is olive green with a white stomach, red lateral spots on its sides, and no spotting on its fins. Being a very predacious fish, it feeds heavily on small fish for its major food source. The construction of a dam on the McCloud, along with the introduction of the brown trout, led to its extirpation from California. Needing very cold water, it couldn't survive the warmer water below the dam or compete with the brown trout, capable of surviving higher temperatures. The last California bull trout was caught in 1975 in the McCloud River. Its disappearance from California is a forewarning other native species can also be lost. (It has recently been listed as *federally threatened* in the western states where it is still found.)

The California record is nine pounds, eleven ounces, caught in the McCloud Reservoir in 1968.

Mountain Whitefish (top), Bull Trout (bottom).

Brook Trout
Salvelinus fontinalis
(Introduced 1871)

The brook trout, which is actually a char, is considered one of the prettiest of all trout. It possesses white, wavy lines on a dark olive-green back, and red spots with blue halos on its sides. The brook trout's origins are eastern United States (thus "eastern brook trout"), including upper Michigan where historically it was a prized native but where today the brown trout dominates many of its native waters. It is also prized throughout the Appalachian Mountains, where it is considered a regional asset. The largest brook trout are found in Labrador where specimens up to six pounds are regularly caught.

In California the brook trout has been widely distributed. Unlike other trout, it is able to propagate in some gravel-bottomed alpine lakes with no tributaries by utilizing springs. With few predators and little fishing pressure, brookies often overpopulate a lake and hence remain small due to the lack of food. In such cases, keeping one's catch actually improves the fishery. Plus, brook trout are among the tastiest of trout. When their numbers are kept in check, brook trout will sometimes grow up to four to five pounds, but they more commonly are less than twelve inches in length and one pound in weight in most California waters.

The state record is nine pounds, twelve ounces, from Silver Lake in Mono County in 1932.

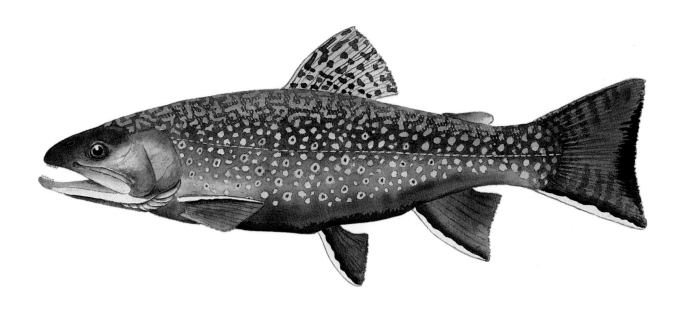

Brook Trout.

Brown Trout
Salmo trutta
(Introduced 1893)

The origins of brown trout are Germany, hence "German Brown trout," and the British Isles, hence "Loch Loven" brown trout. In the United States, it has successfully adapted to become one of the most prevalent wild trout in American waters. Brown trout coloration can vary markedly, from silver to deep orange, with yellow being most common. They are the only California trout with both black and red spots on its body. Highly competitive and aggressive, and prized by anglers, brown trout regularly grow in excess of three to four pounds with favorable conditions. A single large brown trout will sometimes occupy a pool to the domination, even exclusion, of other fish. Given its voracious nature and adaptability, its presence has caused the elimination of native fish in many waters. The brown has adapted especially well in rivers and lakes of the eastern Sierra Nevada, in particular the East Walker River, Hot Creek, the Owens, Crowley Lake, Pleasant Valley Reservoir, and Upper and Lower Twin Lakes near Bridgeport. The Trinity and the McCloud rivers also hold big browns, with the fish in the latter usually being fall spawners.

The California record is twenty-six pounds, eight ounces, caught in Upper Twin Lake in Mono County in 1987.

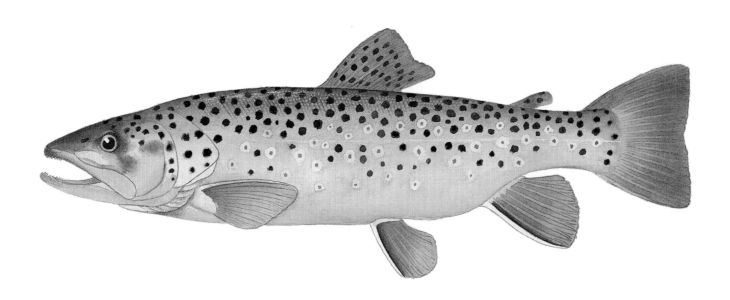

Brown Trout.

Lake Trout (Mackinaw)
Salvelinus namaycush
(Introduced 1889)

First introduced into Lake Tahoe, the lake trout or mackinaw has since been planted in other lakes in the Tahoe region, including Donner Lake. Another member of the char family, the lake trout is one of the least colorful, being gray in color with yellowish gray speckles. It is the only trout in California with large, irregular spots over its entire body. It has a deeply forked tail which distinguishes it from its cousin char, the brook trout. It grows to a large size, with ten pound fish commonly caught, and twenty to thirty pounders taken every season. They are mainly caught by deep trolling.

The California record is thirty-seven pounds, six ounces from Lake Tahoe in 1974.

Arctic Grayling
Thymallus arcticus
(Introduced 1904-1916, and again in the 1970s.)

The distinguishing characteristic of the Arctic grayling is the long, tall dorsal fin with orange and green spotting. It has a steel gray body with random black spots. Several efforts have been made to introduce this fish into California waters, primarily in the first two decades of this century, but they failed. The last lake where graylings existed was Lake Lobdell on the eastern Sierra Nevada. The Arctic grayling is a beautiful and prized game fish in Alaska and Montana, but they didn't adapt to California waters because: 1) they didn't compete well with other trout; 2) they didn't reproduce or survive in waters where they were introduced and thus they had to be reintroduced each year; and 3) the broodstock population used for spawning programs died out and were never replaced.

The state record is one pound, twelve ounces from Lobdell Lake in 1974. (Arctic graylings no longer exist in California waters.)

Lake Trout (top), Arctic Grayling (bottom).

Pacific Salmon

Beyond any other fish, the Pacific salmon are vitally important to human culture in western North America. With remarkable life histories and survival instincts, few other creatures reveal the power and wonder of the natural world as do salmon. Their rapidly declining status underlies some of the most significant issues of river management in the western states.

In California, the chinook or king salmon is the most abundant salmon species (but least abundant throughout other northwestern states), followed by the coho or silver salmon. The other three species—the sockeye, the chum, and the pink—do not have a significant presence in California's waterways except for planted stocks of small, land-locked sockeye or kokanees in a few of the large lakes. Each Pacific salmon species, according to a genetically triggered time, attempts to return to the fresh water where it was born in order to spawn. After spawning, the adult fish die. The decaying salmon carcasses provide rich nutrients to the waterways where their progeny will grow, thus completing one of nature's most remarkable cycles.

The declining health and numbers of wild chinook and coho in California present yet another sad story of habitat degradation. As with other fish species, fishery managers began to rely on hatchery fish to replenish the salmon populations. These too have experienced declines, for without healthy conditions in the river systems, even hatchery stocks are prone to population collapse, especially when an entire stock with limited genetic diversity is located in one place such as a hatchery.

Fish biologists label salmon races by the timing of the adult migration, e.g. winter-run chinook, or by the river system in which they spawn, e.g. Sacramento River spring-run chinook.

The Sacramento River, prime waterway for chinook salmon and many other fish species. Photo by Bob Madgic.

Chinook (King)
Oncorhynchus tshawytscha
(Native; winter-run subspecies is federally and state endangered; spring-run is state threatened.)

The chinook salmon is the largest salmon species, averaging fifteen to twenty-five pounds, and capable of exceeding one hundred pounds. They are distinguished from other salmon species by their body coloration, specifically the spots on the back and tail, and the solid black color of the lower gum line. The rays on the caudal or tail fin are smooth. Reproductive adults are uniformly olive brown to dark maroon; males are darker than females and have a hooked jaw and snout, and an arched back.

There are four runs of chinooks: fall-run, late fall-run, spring-run, and a winter-run subspecies unique to the Sacramento River. Each run is considered to be genetically distinct.

Chinook salmon are all stream spawners, using visual and chemical cues to return to the same water where they were spawned. They require clean gravel, in which the female digs a pit by rolling on her side, with the excavated sand and gravel carried downstream by the current. This leaves a pit or "redd" in which the female deposits her eggs, which are immediately fertilized by a nearby male and then covered up by the female. She moves upstream and repeats the process until all her eggs have been deposited. The flesh of the adult male and female chinooks slowly deteriorates during and after spawning before they eventually die.

Chinook salmon were once abundant in all major river systems in California, with large populations in the many streams of both the Sacramento-San Joaquin and Klamath-Trinity drainages. At mid-century when accurate counting procedures first started, the fall runs of chinook in the Sacramento-San Joaquin river system ranged from 400,000 to 500,000. Runs of a million fish probably occurred earlier in the century. In recent years, the highest number re-entering the Sacramento River system totaled approximately 225,000. In poor years, half that many return.

The Klamath River's fall run early in this century was conservatively estimated at between 300,000 to 400,000 fish, providing the Yurok, Karuk, and Hupa (Hoopa) peoples of the lower Klamath and Trinity rivers with a large portion of their diets as well as being integral to their cultures, including their economies, laws, and religions. Today, the numbers of fall-run salmon have greatly declined, to between 50,000 and 100,000. The large majority of these fish are hatchery salmon instead of the more resilient wild salmon, portending even more future declines if the wild stocks are not replenished.

The largest chinook runs in California historically were the spring-run fish, once totaling more than a million and comprising one of the largest chinook salmon runs on the Pacific Coast. The numbers have steadily decreased, with none left in the San Joaquin River system, and less than a few thousand in the Sacramento River system, mainly in the smaller tributaries to the Sacramento. There are several small, natural runs in the Klamath-Trinity drainage, mostly in the Salmon River.

Late fall-run chinook are found mainly in the Sacramento River. They are the least numerous run in the river, and like the spring-run chinook, their numbers have declined dramatically since counting began in 1967. A small winter run is unique to the Sacramento River. The fall run is now the most abundant, accounting for well over ninety percent of chinook in the Sacramento River system.

The major factors behind the chinook's decline have been the loss of spawning areas due to blockage

The Mokelumne River, like other rivers in the Central Valley, used to have abundant runs of salmon and steelhead. Photo by Bob Madgic.

by dams and steadily degraded habitats below the dams. When Shasta and Keswick dams were built in the 1940s, they denied access to chinook (and steelhead) to prime upstream spawning areas in cold rivers such as the Pit, McCloud, and Sacramento, and affected water temperatures and gravel in the spawning areas left below the dams. The effects of the Red Bluff Diversion Dam have also been highly negative, delaying passage to colder, upstream spawning areas and allowing predators to feast on the out-migrating smolts. (Changing the operation of the dam has recently greatly reduced these problems.) The Friant Dam constructed in 1948 on the San Joaquin along with excessive diversions from the river and its major tributaries so reduced the quantity and quality of water that the spring-run chinook was extirpated from the San Joaquin system. The system now supports only fall-run fish on the Stanislaus, Tuolumne, and Merced, ranging from 10,000 in good years to less than 1,000 in drought years.

Protection for chinook salmon is needed, especially in their freshwater stage, specifically by: 1) providing unimpaired passage of adults to the best available holding and spawning areas; 2) protecting adults in critical habitats; 3) restoring access and habitat in creeks to expand the chinook's range; 4) improving the water quality and quantity in regulated streams for wild salmon; 5) providing sufficient flows for out-migrating juveniles; 6) providing better instream habitat for juvenile fish in the main rivers, especially in the estuary and Delta; 7) properly regulating the harvest of fish; and 8) reducing the effects of hatchery fish on wild populations.

The California record for a chinook is eighty-eight pounds from the Sacramento River in 1979.

Chinook Salmon.

Coho (Silver)
Oncorhynchus kisutch
(Native; federally threatened, state endangered)

Cohos are powerful fish, capable of migrating up waterways other salmon cannot. They are silver in color, hence the name "silver salmon," with small black spots on their backs and the upper lobe of their tail fin. Their tail fin rays are rough compared to the smoothness of the chinook's. Spawning males develop bright red sides and greenish backs, and often grotesquely hooked jaws. The females are paler. Coho do not appear to have the genetically distinct, seasonal runs the more abundant chinook and steelhead trout do.

There used to be more than 500,000 wild coho salmon migrating each year up California rivers. Today, runs number less than 5,000, perhaps even as few as 1,000. Principal populations are located in the Klamath, Trinity, Mad, Noyo, and Eel rivers. Hatchery-reared coho (and chinook) salmon have been stocked in large reservoirs such as Berryessa, Almanor, Shasta, and Oroville, with considerable success although they must be restocked annually to support angling.

Coho salmon are smaller than the chinook, averaging six to thirteen pounds, and spawn in smaller streams than chinooks. They typically return to their home streams as three-year-olds, having spent a year in the stream where they were born, and a couple of years in the ocean. Because of their extended residence in coastal streams where they seek out deep, cold, and well shaded pools, with plenty of overhead cover, they are more vulnerable to the effects of erosion, logging, dams, and drought. Their drastic decline in California signals a decline in water quality and watershed health. The key to the coho salmon's future is the protection of their spawning and rearing streams, and the restoration of their damaged habitat.

The state record is twenty-two pounds, caught in Paper Mill Creek, Marin County, 1959.

Coho Salmon.

Sockeye or Kokanee
Oncorhynchus nerka
(Sockeye, native; Kokanee, introduced 1941)

This salmon is known throughout the Northwest and Alaska as a "sockeye" where it is anadromous. Small numbers of wild sockeye are sometimes observed in California streams, most likely strays from the Northwest. In contrast to other salmon species, sockeye migration runs are restricted to river systems with lakes accessible to salmon. Sockeye are plankton feeders, thus their young require lakes where they feed on plankton before migrating to the ocean.

The subspecies more available in California's waters is called a kokanee. It is planted in lakes where it spends its entire life "landlocked" as a game fish. A kokanee is identical in shape and color to the anadromous sockeye, except it is much smaller. It has silver sides with a bluish back (hence it is sometimes called a "blueback") and almost no spots. It is often thought to be a rainbow trout, but the kokanee has a longer anal fin and smaller scales that tend to rub off easily. In some lakes where the fish are abundant, kokanee seldom exceed twelve inches in length and less than a pound in weight; in others it reaches nineteen inches in length and two to three pounds in weight. The difference is due to the quantity of available food and the competition for it.

The state record is four pounds, thirteen ounces, caught in Lake Tahoe in 1973.

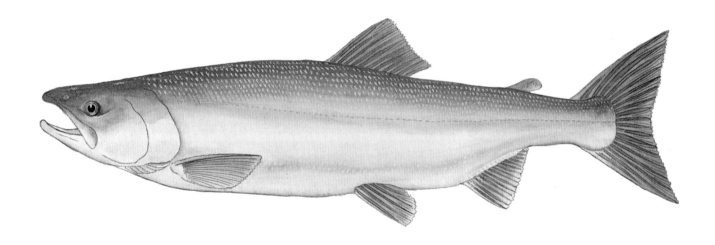

Kokanee Salmon.

Pink Salmon
Oncorhynchus gorbuscha
(Native)

Pink salmon are extremely rare in California, the southern edge of their range. Although they may have occurred in noticeable numbers in the past, most fish recorded in the state today are probably fish that strayed while at sea and followed other salmon species upstream. Smaller than other anadromous salmon, pinks average only two to five pounds. They are readily distinguished by the large oval spots on their backs and tail fins. Spawning males develop a large hump on their backs, thereby also being named "humpback" salmon.

No state record has been recorded.

Chum
Oncorhynchus keta
(Native)

Chum salmon are the second largest Pacific salmon species, weighing up to forty pounds. They can be distinguished from other salmon (except sockeye) by the absence of black spots on the back and fins. Spawning males develop reddish vertical bars on their sides; females have a reddish lateral band. Chum salmon do not migrate far inland to spawn, not being good swimmers like their cousins. They will spend from four to seven years at sea before migrating to fresh water.

Of all the Pacific salmons, chum salmon had the widest natural geographical distribution, historically ranging from the Mackenzie River on the Canadian Arctic coast of North America down to California. Formerly found in waters from Sacramento northward, they are rarely encountered in California today. It appears the only California rivers currently used by chum salmon for spawning are the South Fork Trinity, Klamath, and Smith rivers, although the numbers of fish in each river are small. Its survival in California is at risk, and it is in danger of extinction.

No state record has been recorded.

Pink Salmon (top), Chum Salmon (bottom).

Clear Lake, California's largest natural lake, is home to many fish species. DFG photo by Rick Macedo.

Warmwater Game Fish.

California has an abundance of lakes and reservoirs supporting varied fish species. Most of the warmwater game species live in still waters, i.e. ponds and lakes, although some are found in rivers and streams. In still water, certain physical factors must be present to support a healthy fishery, including: dissolved oxygen, varied water temperatures supportive of differing fish species, carbon dioxide, calcium, and nutrients (e.g. nitrates, phosphates, silicates). Aquatic biota in the form of algae and aquatic vascular plants, invertebrates, and small fish provide food sources for larger aquatic organisms higher in the food chain.

Warmwater fish tend to maintain the full "biotic potential" of any body of water, meaning the total weight of such fishes will remain nearly constant, and close to the maximum the body of water is capable of supporting. Therefore, the fewer the fish, the larger they will be; conversely, the more fish, the smaller. The key factor in determining the biomass of fish is the amount of food available. If the food supplies are insufficient, growth rates within the fish population will be reduced and stunting may occur. When warmwater fishes have become established in suitable bodies of water, "maintenance stocking" of small fish is generally not beneficial since most species are able to maintain themselves in the absence of unusual conditions causing fish kills.

With the exception of only one species—the Sacramento perch—all warmwater game fish in California have been introduced, often with disastrous results for the state's native species. Man's recreational interests have often superseded his interest in preserving ecological integrity. And since many of California's lakes are man-created reservoirs, other issues for fish productivity and management arise. For instance, high levels of algae may be beneficial for fish but detrimental to drinking water sources. Chemicals to reduce the algae in a reservoir will often reduce the numbers of fish by altering the food chain. Fluctuating water levels and the steep sides of many reservoirs often reduce spawning success and impair food production for fish.

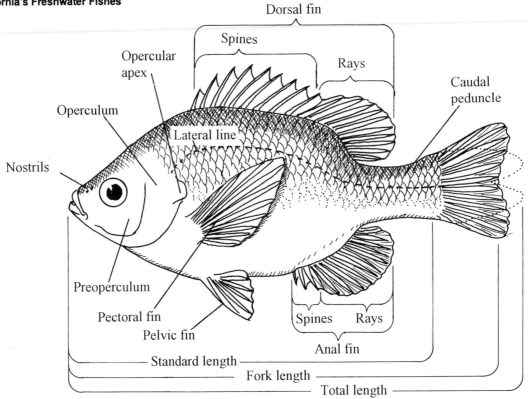

Dorsal fin

Spines

Rays

Caudal peduncle

Opercular apex

Operculum

Lateral line

Nostrils

Preoperculum

Pectoral fin

Pelvic fin

Spines   Rays

Anal fin

Standard length

Fork length

Total length

External Anatomy of Warmwater Fish.

Lake Morena in southeastern San Diego County has rocky shoreline, productive habitat for warmwater fish. Photo by Richard Alden Bean.

Sunfish Family

This fish family includes more game fish than any other freshwater family in North America. Many anglers started out by catching sunfish as children, particularly bluegills and pumpkinseeds. In California, the members of the sunfish family are: Sacramento perch, bluegill, redear sunfish, green sunfish, warmouth, pumpkinseed, black crappie, white crappie, redeye bass, largemouth bass, smallmouth bass, and spotted bass. The native Sacramento perch has largely been extirpated from its original waters. Members of the sunfish family are nesting fishes. The male scoops out a depression or nest and one or more females deposit their eggs. The male then guards the eggs and the newly hatched young fish for many days.

Sacramento Perch
Archoplites interruptus
(Native; special concern)

Sacramento perch are the only native sunfish west of the Rocky Mountains. They are deep bodied fish that are brownish on the top and upper sides, with a metallic green to purplish sheen on the sides, dark vertical bars, and a white underside. They typically are eight to twelve inches in size (although they are capable of growing in excess of twenty inches), and are good tasting fish. Historically they were found in sloughs, slow-moving rivers (e.g. the Sacramento-San Joaquin, the Pajaro, and the Salinas river systems), in the lakes of the Central Valley, and in Clear Lake. Although a few still occupy Clear Lake, they have been largely extirpated from their native waters, and are found only in a few reservoirs and farm ponds where they tolerate a wide range of water conditions, including warm, turbid, and moderately alkaline waters. They are seldom able to coexist with non-native sunfishes, catfish, or carp which eat the perch's eggs. A productive sport fishery for Sacramento perch exists in Crowley Lake where they were illegally introduced in the 1960s. Since all reservoirs have a finite life due to silting, they do not provide long-term environments for the fish in them. In order to develop a stable population of Sacramento perch, they should be established in suitable habitats without other sunfishes, and valued as a sport fish. In farm ponds they must be heavily harvested to prevent stunting.

The state record catch stands at three pounds, ten ounces from Crowley Lake in 1979.

Sacramento Perch.

Green Sunfish
Lepomis cyanellus
(Introduced 1891)

The green sunfish possesses a relatively large mouth for a sunfish, extending beyond the front of the eye, with iridescent blue-green markings on body and head (thus "green" sunfish). It reproduces in abundance, often producing stunted populations. They spawn in shallow water in colonies. The male guards the saucer-shaped nest after the female deposits her eggs, numbering in the thousands. Coupled with a vigorous aggressiveness in defending its territory, this fish will not only dominate a stream pool, but become its only inhabitant, often displacing native fish. It is thus not a good occupant for a farm pond or stream. It possesses a high tolerance for warm and shallow waters, with low oxygen content and high alkalinity. Green sunfish rarely exceed seven inches.

California record: One pound, twelve ounces from a farm pond near Bella Vista, Shasta County, in 1978.

Warmouth
Lepomis gulosus
(Introduced 1891)

This fish closely resembles the green sunfish in behavior, size, and shape, and in its shallow water habitat. It prefers weed beds and soft bottoms, and is more tolerant of muddy water than most species. It will also seek out stumps, and has been called a "stumpknocker." Its coloration is yellowish brown. Teeth on its tongue separates it from all other sunfishes. Less aggressive than the green sunfish, it is also less abundant since it gives way to its green cousin. It is most prevalent in the Central Valley, especially around Turlock. Although they rarely reach more than ten inches in length, they are good eating.

The state record is twelve ounces, caught in the American River in Sacramento County in 1982.

Green Sunfish (top), Warmouth (bottom).

Bluegill
Lepomis macrochirus
(Introduced 1908)

The bluegill has a blue-black flap at the rear of its gill (thus "blue" gill), vertical bars on its sides, and a small mouth. It is one of the most abundant sunfish in California and a major competitor to the Sacramento perch. The bluegill is found in virtually all warmwater lakes, and in warm, slow-moving streams. They can adapt to varied waters, and reproduce in high numbers. They grow so numerous in some lakes and ponds that they become stunted in size, a characteristic of fishes overpopulating their environment. The bluegill feeds along the shoreline and when in schools can be readily caught by the angler. They prefer quiet, weedy water in which to feed and hide. This is one fish that anglers should keep, not only to reduce the population but also because they are good tasting. Bluegills over ten inches long are uncommon.

The California record is three pounds, eight ounces, caught in 1991 in Lower Otay Reservoir.

Pumpkinseed
Lepomis gibbosus
(Introduced 1918)

The pumpkinseed possesses a spot of orange or red on the lower part of its opercular lobe (thus "pumpkinseed"). Its cheeks have prominent blue and orange stripes. The pumpkinseed feeds in the inshore zone, mainly on the bottom, with snails its preferred food. It prefers cool climates, thus being found more in northern California and northern states. Populations frequently consist of "stunted" fish, less than four inches long, thus they are not a good fish for California waters and of little interest to anglers.

The California record is one pound from Mountain Meadows Reservoir in Lassen County, 1996.

Bluegill (top), Pumpkinseed (bottom).

Redear Sunfish
Lepomis microlophus
(Introduced 1951)

The redear sunfish has a broad red or orange margin below and behind the opercular lobe (thus "red" ear), and long and pointed pectoral fins. It feeds along the bottom in deep water, and it deposits fewer eggs and produces fewer offspring than the bluegill, breeding at three or four years of age compared to the bluegill which often breeds as a yearling. The populations of this sunfish are apt to be smaller than the bluegill's, but with bigger fish, in the nine to twelve inch range. It makes a good species for farm ponds.

The state record is five pounds, three ounces, taken in 1994 from the Folsom South Canal.

Redeye Bass
Micropterus coosae
(Introduced 1953)

The redeye bass possesses red fins and eyes (thus "redeye"). It is the smallest of the bass species, rarely over 14 inches, and has generally not thrived in California waters. It is a stream fish imported from the southeastern United States, and is similar to trout in feeding habits and habitat requirements. Where it has managed to secure a foothold in the lower elevation of mountain streams, it has probably been to the detriment of the native fishes through competition and predation. It does not compete well with other bass species.

There is no recorded state record for a redeye bass.

Redear Sunfish (top), Redeye Bass (bottom).

Largemouth Bass
Micropterus salmoides
(Introduced 1874)

The largemouth bass, also called a black bass, is one of the most popular and prized warmwater game fishes in California and the nation. It is present in nearly all suitable lakes, sloughs, slow moving rivers, and farm ponds in California. Clear Lake has a rich black bass fishery; so too do most of the state's reservoirs.

The largemouth bass has a dark, blotchy, continuous longitudinal band on its sides with a deeply notched dorsal fin. They are readily distinguished from other black basses in that their upper jaw extends past a vertical line drawn through the rear margin of the eye (thus "largemouth"). They prefer warm water, around 80° F. When the water drops below 50° F, they descend to deep water and become inactive. Largemouth bass are among the best fighting fish, hitting lures and baits hard, and fighting tenaciously.

While the average size of this gamefish is twelve to fifteen inches in length and one to three pounds in weight, and smaller in ponds, it is capable of growing much larger. Hookups with largemouth bass over three pounds are what make this fish such a popular quarry for anglers.

The state record is twenty-one pounds, twelve ounces from Lake Castaic, Los Angeles County, in 1991.

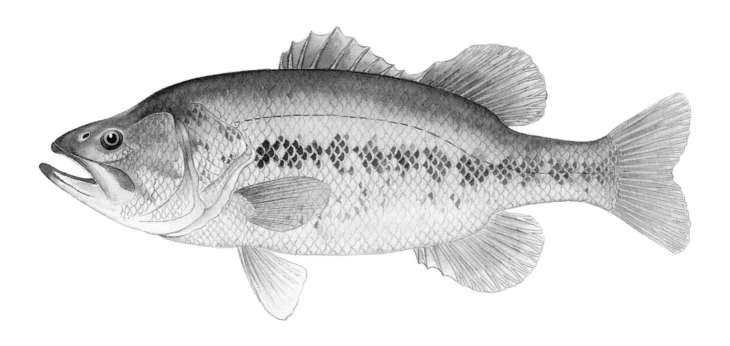

Largemouth Bass.

Smallmouth Bass
Micropterus dolomieu
(Introduced 1874)

Smallmouth bass have dark vertical bars on their sides. In contrast to the largemouth bass, they do not have a deeply notched dorsal fin and their upper jaw does not extend to the rear margin of the eye (thus "smallmouth"). Smallmouth bass prefer lower temperatures (less than 75° F) and swifter currents than largemouth bass. They do best in clear, boulder-strewn streams with large pools, and in clear lakes and reservoirs with scant vegetation and rocky shoals for spawning. They are abundant in many Sierra Nevada foothill rivers and in many reservoirs, particularly Shasta, Ruth, and Trinity reservoirs.

In contrast to many other fish species, it is the male smallmouth bass that builds the spawning nest. After fanning out the stones and gravel with its tail, the male selects a female ripe with eggs, and drives her to the nest. Once she deposits her eggs, he will select one or two more females to repeat the process.

Some anglers consider smallmouth to be even better fighters than largemouth bass, and better tasting, but they are generally smaller, seldom over three pounds. Most catches can be expected to be in the twelve-inch, one-pound class. They are often found in rivers near where they empty into lakes or reservoirs. Trout fishing techniques work well with the smallmouth.

The state record is nine pounds, one ounce, caught in Trinity Lake, Trinity County, 1976.

Smallmouth Bass.

Spotted Bass
Micropterus punctulatus
(Introduced 1973)

The spotted bass closely resembles the largemouth bass. However, its upper jaw extends only to the rear margin of the eye, the dark lateral band is blotchy and not continuous, and the dorsal fin is not deeply notched. Imported from the southern states, the spotted bass has done well in California due to its deep water spawning tendencies. (It is the Alabama spotted bass that has become the preferred variety of spotted bass in California since it grows larger than its cousin in the Mississippi drainage—the source of the original spotted bass plants in California.) When water levels of reservoirs fluctuate, fish such as largemouth bass that spawn along the shores will have their eggs dewatered depending upon drawdown. Spotted bass are more successful reproducing in lakes such as Lake Shasta where the level drops precipitously as the summer progresses, thus developing abundant populations of mature fish in the two to three pound class in many of the state's reservoirs. They are becoming one of California's most popular game fish.

The state record is nine pounds, seven ounces, taken from Pine Flat Reservoir, Fresno County, in 1994.

Spotted Bass.

Black Crappie
Pomoxis nigromaculatus
(Introduced 1891)

The black crappie is silvery in color with irregular dark green or black spots (thus "black" crappie). It possesses a large mouth, and eats zooplankton, aquatic insects, and small fish. It does better in clear reservoirs than its cousin, the white crappie. Both species will congregate in highly localized schools, often around submerged objects. Black crappie have an extremely high reproductive rate, and need abundant forage, cover, and heavy harvesting for a desirable fishery to exist. Without heavy cropping, they tend to overpopulate and become stunted. Fish over fifteen inches are uncommon. Clear Lake in Lake County and Lake Britton in Shasta County at times produce outstanding crappie fishing.

The California record is four pounds, one ounce, caught in New Hogan Lake, Calaveras County, in 1975.

White Crappie
Pomoxis annularis
(Introduced 1891)

The white crappie is silvery white in color (thus "white" crappie), with spotted vertical bars on its sides. It possesses the same basic behavior and environmental needs as the black crappie except it is more frequently found in warmer and more turbid water, particularly river sloughs. White crappie are most abundant in the waters of San Diego County, and in the Colorado River drainage. Overall, they are less abundant than the black crappie. Both species commonly weigh in at half to three-quarters of a pound when caught, although occasionally one weighing up to three pounds is brought to the angler's net.

The state record stands at four pounds, eight ounces from Clear Lake, Lake County, in 1971.

Black Crappie (top), White Crappie (bottom).

The Sacramento-San Joaquin Delta is one of the richest fish habitats in the country. Department of Water Resources photo.

Temperate Bass Family

Striped Bass
Morone saxatilis
(Introduced 1879)

Striped bass are steel blue to olive green on their tops, with a series of seven to eight horizontal, continuous blackish stripes along their sides, and white bellies. Their large scales give off a faint brass colored tint. A prized game fish in California, the striped bass is an anadromous fish with the singular ability to move freely between fresh and salt water—from sea through estuaries up rivers, and then back again—without a triggering cause such as the spawning urge in salmonids. Native to the Atlantic coast, it was introduced into California in the Sacramento-San Joaquin Delta in 1879 as a food fish. It was so success-ful that it once supported a thriving commercial fish-ery at the end of the nineteenth century, averaging over one million pounds of fish per year. This business ended in 1935, and the fish today is pursued strictly for its sporting qualities.

Stripers spend most of their time in the ocean, entering the Delta and Sacramento and San Joaquin rivers in the spring to spawn. They can be found in the ocean from below the California southern border up to Vancouver Island. The largest populations today are centered in the San Joaquin-Sacramento Estuary, in particular San Francisco Bay. Several water bodies contain self-sustaining landlocked populations of striped bass, including San Luis Reservoir in Merced County, Black Butte Reservoir in Tehama and Glenn counties, Camp Far West Reservoir in Yuba and Placer counties, Lake Pillsbury in Lake County, and Millerton Lake in Madera and Fresno counties.

The number of striped bass has been dwindling in the past thirty years, and could fall to levels that threaten their future in California. During all but very high runoff years, a major portion of the flow in the Sacramento-San Joaquin River Delta, along with a high proportion of the striped bass eggs and larvae, are sucked into the giant state and federal water pumps at Tracy that transport water to central and southern California. To prevent this, the Department of Water Resources and the Bureau of Reclamation have constructed fish screens. These screens, how-ever, have not been very effective. The situation is expected to worsen as future pumping increases. The heavy pumping also creates a flow reversal damaging to striped bass as well as other fishes. The DFG and a consortium of fishery groups have developed a rescue plan whereby striped bass are recaptured at the pumps and transported to net pens in the Lower Delta where the young fish are kept for one to two years to gain sufficient size and strength to resist the suction of the aqueducts of the pumps. These fish would be wild and therefore of higher value than hatchery-bred fish. As of 1998 the project was in the experimental stage and of a very small scale.

The minimum size for keeping a striped bass is eighteen inches, and most fish caught will be under thirty inches. But because striped bass can live long lives, in excess of twenty years, specimens can reach fifty inches in length, and fifty pounds in weight.

The California record is sixty-seven pounds, eight ounces, caught in O'Neill Forebay in Merced County, in 1992.

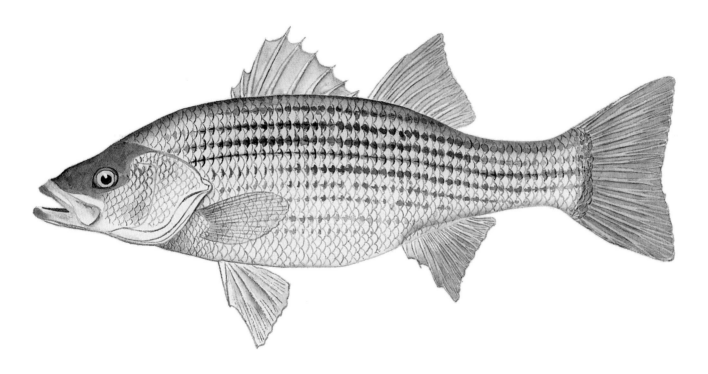

Striped Bass.

White Bass
Morone chrysops
(Introduced 1967)

The white bass has interrupted black horizontal stripes on its silver body. Its body depth is deeper than the striped bass. Although the white bass is in the same family as the striped bass, it lives in fresh water exclusively. It was originally introduced into Nacimiento Reservoir in 1965 where it became established as a good game fish. However, this voracious fish was illegally placed in Kaweah Reservoir in Tulare County, from where it could escape to the San Joaquin River and hence the Delta, threatening striped bass and chinook salmon populations. The Kaweah Reservoir population was chemically eradicated during the early 1980s.

The maximum length for a white bass is about eighteen inches, and its maximum weight is about five and a half pounds. The state record is five pounds, five ounces taken from Ferguson Lake (Colorado River) in 1972.

The Perch Family

Yellow Perch
Perca flavescens
(Introduced 1891)

The yellow perch has a yellow or olive body (thus "yellow" perch), with six to eight dark vertical bands. In states where it is native, the yellow perch is considered a good eating and sport fish even though it seldom exceeds twelve inches in length. A school-oriented species, yellow perch can become overpopulated and stunted in waters originally containing prolific food sources. They are mainly found in Copco Lake and Iron Gate Reservoir, and the quieter waters of the Klamath River, all in northeastern California. Since yellow perch pose a threat to California's native species, including cold water salmonids, fish biologists view their presence here as undesirable.

In California the only other member of the perch family is the bigscale logperch, also an introduced species, and a member of a subgroup known as "darters."

There is no recorded state record for a yellow perch.

White Bass (top), Yellow Perch (bottom).

The Catfish Family

All seven species of catfish (brown bullhead, yellow bullhead, black bullhead, white catfish, channel catfish, flathead catfish, blue catfish) have been introduced to California, and occupy a variety of both warm and cold waters—from muddy ponds to fast moving rivers. Bullheads have been placed in cold mountain lakes where they grow abundant while remaining small, competing with trout for forage. Once they become established, they are almost impossible to remove except through repeated chemical treatment.

Catfish lack scales so their sides are smooth. A distinguishing feature is the sharp, slightly poisonous spines in their back and side fins, capable of producing a painful incision to the careless handler. They possess eight long "whiskers" or feelers around their mouths, thus the name "catfish." Six of these whiskers hanging lowest are called "barbels." Catfish are pervasive nighttime feeders, and engorge all kinds of foods, including dead and rotten matter.

White Catfish
Ameiurus catus
(Introduced 1874)

The white catfish is the most abundant catfish in California, occupying most of the Central Valley waters. More than ninety percent of the catfish caught in the Sacramento-San Joaquin Delta are white catfish. They are bluish to black on their tops, silvery on their undersides, with white barbels (thus "white" catfish). Their tails are slightly forked. Capable of reaching twelve pounds in weight, they prefer slow, large rivers. Clear Lake in Lake County has a large population.

The state record is twenty-two pounds, caught in William Land Park Pond, Sacramento County, in 1994. (This fish was reared in a fish hatchery and planted in this small urban park soon before it was caught. The previous record was a wild fish of fifteen pounds caught in the Delta in 1951.)

White Catfish.

Brown Bullhead
Ameiurus nebulosus
(Introduced 1874)

The brown bullhead is the most widely distributed member of the catfish family. It and other bullhead species are so named because of their pronounced head size relative to the rest of their bodies. It possesses a dark brown back (thus "brown" bullhead) with a yellowish to gray underside. Sides may be slightly mottled. The tail is squarish. They occupy the deep waters of lakes and slow rivers and can grow up to two pounds. As a result of illegal introductions in trout lakes, they quickly became overpopulated and stunted, creating detrimental competition with trout and a nuisance for anglers.

The California state record for a "bullhead" is four pounds, eight ounces, caught in Trinity Lake, Trinity County, in 1993.

Black Bullhead
Ameiurus melas
(Introduced 1940)

The black bullhead resembles the brown bullhead without the mottled coloring on the sides. Its coloration can be yellow-brown to black (thus "black" bullhead). In California it is capable of growing up to eighteen inches in length and two pounds in weight. Its barbs on the side fins are not as sharp as with other catfish species. Populations in high elevation lakes are frequently stunted.

The black bullhead has a high tolerance for warm water (up to 75° F), low oxygen, and high carbon dioxide levels. Thus it can exist in warm backwater sections of lakes and in small, shallow ponds, lakes, and sloughs. Parent black bullheads are especially attentive to their young, thus making them excellent subjects for observation. Since they often remain small, they make good fish for home aquariums.

No separate state record has been recorded.

Brown Bullhead (top), Black Bullhead (bottom).

Yellow Bullhead
Ameiurus natalis
(Introduced 1940)

The yellow bullhead is not a widely distributed or popular fish in California, since it prefers permanent, warm streams with good oxygen levels, a type of water not readily available in the Golden State. It exists mainly in the shallower sections of the Colorado River. It is also found in the shallow bays of some reservoirs, preferring clear water with lots of vegetation. Its back is usually yellow-brown to black, and the belly somewhat yellow (thus "yellow" bullhead). The tail is rounded. It seldom exceeds two pounds in weight.

No separate state record has been recorded.

Flathead Catfish
Pylodictis olivaris
(Introduced 1962)

The flathead is distinguished by dark brown mottling on its back and upper sides, its broad, flattened head (thus "flathead" catfish), and its longer lower jaw compared to its upper jaw. It has a squarish tail, and the fewest rays (14 to 17 on the anal fin) of all catfish species. A midwestern native, it was introduced to the Colorado River from where it found its way to the canals of the Imperial Valley. It strongly prefers to reside in deep pools, and to feed mainly at night. As a result they are not easily taken by an angler. The flathead catfish can attain lengths of fifty-five inches, and weights in excess of seventy pounds.

The state record is sixty pounds, caught in the Colorado River, Palo Verde Lagoon, in 1992.

Yellow Bullhead (top), Flathead Catfish (bottom).

Channel Catfish
Ictalurus punctatus
(Introduced 1891)

The channel catfish thrives in some large reservoirs in southern California, in the Colorado River, and in portions of the Sacramento River drainage, particularly the Sutter Bypass. It can grow in excess of fifty pounds. Its outstanding eating qualities combined with its size and good fighting spirit make it a prized sport fish. Sometimes confused with the blue and white catfish, the channel catfish has a more deeply forked tail and irregular spotting than the white catfish, and fewer rays in the anal fin (24 to 29) compared to the blue catfish (30-35).

Channel catfish are an excellent fish to raise artificially since they readily eat commercial foods and grow rapidly and large. They possess an outstanding ability to survive in waters where they are placed in contrast to the high mortality rates experienced by other fish species, making it a preferred fish for commercial production in fish farms as a food source. They are stocked in many urban lakes and ponds for "put and take" fishing opportunities.

The state record is fifty-two pounds, ten ounces, caught in the Santa Ana River Lakes, Orange County, 1993.

Blue Catfish
Ictalurus furcatus
(Introduced 1869)

The blue catfish is the largest of all American catfishes, reaching lengths of sixty inches and weights of over one hundred pounds. Its adult body is bluish on top (thus "blue" catfish) and white below. Its anal fin possesses the most rays of all catfishes (30 to 35), and it is the longest as well, extending for one third the length of its body. The blue catfish is found primarily in the reservoirs of San Diego County: Lake Jennings, Lake Mathews, El Capitan Reservoir, Otay Reservoir, and Sutherland Reservoir. More than other catfish, it grows increasingly piscivorus in its eating habits, preferring live fishes and crayfish over dead matter.

California record: eighty-two pounds, one ounce, from Lower Otay Reservoir in 1996.

Channel Catfish (top), Blue Catfish (bottom).

The Sturgeon Family

Included among California's native fishes is the largest freshwater fish in the world—the sturgeon—an ancient fish not resembling any other species. Sturgeons grow slowly and live long lives, up to one hundred years. They have a unique structure and appearance. Rows of bony shields or plates partly cover the head and body. Their eyes are small. The mouth is on the underside of the head. A row of four rubbery whiskers or feelers is on the front of the mouth. In eating, the sturgeon extends its mouth and sucks the food up from the bottom much like a vacuum cleaner.

In the 1880s, the annual commercial catch of white sturgeon in California reached 700,000 pounds. But a combination of overharvesting, dams, and pollution almost caused the fish to disappear. Since 1954, only sport fishing for this unique creature is legal. The sturgeon is a prized game fish due to its size and tasty flesh, and eggs from which caviar is made. However, their numbers can suffer from overfishing if the fishery is not carefully managed.

White Sturgeon
Acipenser transmontanus
(Native)

The white sturgeon is capable of reaching lengths of twenty feet and weights over 1,000 pounds, with some individuals weighing close to 2,000 pounds. Its coloration is grayish brown fading to white on its undersides (thus "white" sturgeon). The lateral plates number 38-48 in a single row. It lives primarily in estuaries before moving up large rivers such as the Sacramento, San Joaquin, and Klamath in late winter and early spring to spawn.

After spawning, both the female and male adults leave the eggs clinging to vegetation and other bottom matter to survive on their own. The eggs hatch in three to seven days with the baby sturgeon living on the egg yolks. They then consume tiny animal life in the water, growing from less than an inch to five inches in a month, on their way to becoming the world's largest freshwater fish.

The Sacramento-San Joaquin Delta holds the largest population of white sturgeon in the state. The California record is 468 pounds, taken in San Pablo Bay in 1983.

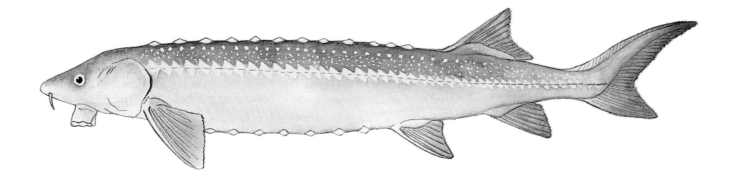

White Sturgeon.

Green Sturgeon
Acipenser medirostris
(Native; special concern)

The green sturgeon is a much smaller species, and less common, than the white sturgeon. It reaches maximum lengths of seven feet and weights of 350 pounds. It possesses an olive-green body color with an obscure green strip on its lower side (thus "green" sturgeon). The plates in the lateral row number 23-30 in a double row. In contrast to the white sturgeon, the green sturgeon is not considered a good food fish. They therefore have not attracted much attention or study beyond Native Americans who have netted green sturgeon for food since historical times.

More of a marine species, the green sturgeon will travel long distances in the ocean. It seldom moves past the estuaries of large rivers, with the exception of the Sacramento, Klamath, and Trinity rivers where they sometimes swim far upriver, as far as Happy Camp on the Klamath and Red Bluff on the Sacramento. They appear to spawn only in the Sacramento and Klamath river systems. The Feather River, a major tributary of the Sacramento, may be a prime spawning ground. The depositing of eggs and growing patterns of the young fish closely follow that of their white cousins.

Green sturgeon potentially are in trouble worldwide, with declining numbers probable in waters where they historically lived, such as those off of Japan, Russia, and Canada. Since they have not been a popular game or food fish, little is known about their actual status and thus few efforts have been undertaken to ensure their future.

No separate state record has been recorded.

Green Sturgeon.

The Herring-Shad Family

Although this family of fishes possesses economic importance throughout the world, mainly as a marine species, it is not so in California. Two species have been introduced to California with decidedly different results. The first is the American Shad which has become one of California's best sporting fishes. The second member of this family is threadfin shad, a small, silvery non-game fish introduced in lakes and reservoirs to provide a food source for larger game fish in California lakes and reservoirs. Instead it often competes for zooplankton in many waters with native fishes. (For threadfin shad see page 154.)

American Shad
Alosa sapidissima
(Introduced 1871)

The American shad is a silvery fish with a thin, deep body, and a sharp, sawlike keel along the length of its belly. It has several small spots along the lateral line behind its head. An anadromous species, the American shad is native to the Atlantic coast. It was the first fish to be introduced to California, primarily as a source of food. The fry were dumped in the Sacramento River, and they later headed out to the Pacific Ocean where they grew and matured, returning to the river after three to five years to spawn. Their fighting abilities, and good size (three to four pounds), make them a popular game fish. The shad runs occur from April to July, mainly in the Sacramento River and its tributaries, and to a lesser extent in the Russian and Klamath rivers.

The California record is seven pounds, five ounces, taken from the Feather River, Butte County, in 1985.

American Shad.

Non-Game Fish

Many species of fish not valued by humans for their sporting or food qualities have long populated California's diverse waters. Before these species were recognized as serving crucial ecological functions, little attention was given to their preservation. In fact, misguided efforts attempted to eradicate many of these native species from trout waters, including presumed "competitors" like tui chubs and suckers, or predators like squawfish. With recognition now that biological diversity is crucial for maintaining the health of the planet, the vital nature of each and every species has become accepted and forms the basis for the state and federal endangered species acts. Thus obscure fish, such as the tui chub, stickleback, and the hitch, are now given the importance, at least by scientists and many government officials, formerly reserved for game fish.

In addition to game fish, the state introduced alien non-game fish, usually for specific purposes. What purposes? To provide forage for game fish, e.g. golden shiners; to carry out a function within nature, e.g. western mosquitofish for mosquito control; or to provide a commercial market, e.g. carp.

For many of these fish, there may be several related species and subspecies. In this guide, only one fish is illustrated as representative of the species. In the following pages, native species are presented first, followed by five introduced fish.

*Varied subspecies of the remarkable pupfish occupy water in arid settings such as
the Cottonball Marsh in Death Valley. DFG photo by Betsy Bolster.*

California Roach
Hesperoleucus symmetricus
(Native; special concern)

Next to the speckled dace, the California roach is the most widely distributed native minnow in California. Its head and eyes are large, its mouth small and low. The dorsal fin is set well back. Many subspecies of the roach are found in the Sacramento, San Joaquin, and upper Pit river drainages, the Russian River, and coastal streams. It is primarily a minnow of tributary streams. Even though these streams may lose their volume as the summer progresses, this fish can still survive in the remaining shallow, warm pools. Few other species can survive under these habitat conditions.

The California roach rarely exceeds five inches in length.

Delta Smelt
Hypomesus transpacificus
(Native; threatened)

The Delta smelt is a small, trim, silvery fish with a small mouth not reaching beyond the middle of the eye. It lives in large schools, and occupies the lower reaches of the Sacramento-San Joaquin Delta. The presence of a small adipose fin as the second dorsal fin is the best single characteristic of the smelt to distinguish it from the introduced inland silverside. The Delta smelt is an important forage fish for larger fish species. They live a short life, dying after spawning, mostly in their second year. Its one-year life cycle makes this species a good barometer of conditions for many other species, such as striped bass. Delta smelt populations have declined more than ninety percent since the 1970s. Increased water diversions from the Delta and dredging of Delta channels has drastically reduced freshwater outflow to Suisun Bay and eliminated the shallow upstream habitat of the Delta smelt.

The average size of the Delta smelt is two to three inches.

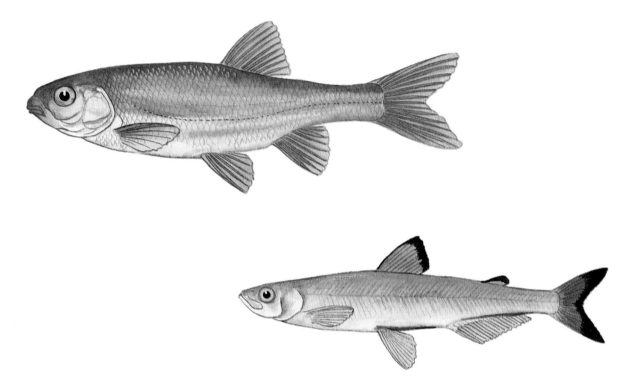

California Roach (top), Delta Smelt (bottom).

Hitch
Lavinia exilicauda
(Native)

The hitch is a minnow of the slower, deeper waters of streams, sloughs, and reservoirs. Juvenile fish will occupy the nearshore, shallow-water habitat before moving to deeper waters after maturing. It possesses a small and conical head with a small mouth, and large scales. The anal fin is longer and higher than that of most other native minnows. Hitch was a food source for Native Americans, and it remains today an important food source for other fish, birds, and varied mammals. (The Clear Lake hitch, a declining subspecies, is classed as a *species of special concern.*)

Hitch can reach lengths of fourteen inches.

Lahontan Redside
Richardsonius egregius
(Native)

The Lahontan redside, a strikingly beautiful minnow, is one of the smallest minnows. A dark stripe along its side is a distinguishing characteristic. During the spawning season, it has a reddish band. The Lahontan redside is found widely in lakes and streams within the drainages of the Truckee, Carson, and Walker rivers. It occupies the inshore areas of waters where it feeds on a variety of insect larvae and other aquatic invertebrates. It has been introduced to higher elevation lakes from the American River northward where it has adversely affected trout in some areas.

The Lahontan redside rarely exceeds three inches.

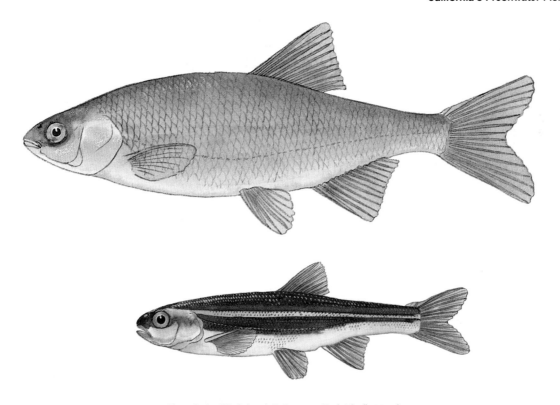

Clear Lake Hitch (top), Lahontan Redside (bottom).

Pacific lamprey
Lampetra tridentata
River lamprey
Lampetra ayresi
(Natives)

Lampreys are the most primitive form of living vertebrates, representing a special species of jawless vertebrates with cartilaginous skeletons in contrast to the bony structure of other freshwater fish species. They possess long, round, eel-like bodies, slimy to the touch. The largest subspecies is the Pacific lamprey, an anadromous, parasitic fish that attaches itself to the sides of its host fish, such as a salmon, and then sucks fluids from the host for its sustenance. It will move into estuaries, and then migrate upstream to spawn, much like salmon. The young, called ammocoetes, live in the soft-bottom habitat of stream backwaters for four to seven years before metamorphosing into adults. California's Native American tribes looked to the lamprey as a major source of food. Some kinds of lampreys live their entire lives in rivers and streams and are not parasitic.

The Pacific lamprey can reach lengths of twenty-five inches, while the river lamprey does not exceed thirteen inches.

Desert pupfish
Cyprinodon macularius
(Native; see below for status of the subspecies of pupfish.)

The pupfish is a small desert fish of the killifish family, capable of surviving in extreme habitat conditions, including high water temperatures in excess of 110° F, high salinity (four times that of sea water), and low oxygen levels. No other freshwater fish species can live under these conditions, thereby making the pupfish a unique creature with the rarest of physiological make-ups. Pupfish possess a small mouth with scissorlike teeth, a short and rounded snout, and very large scales. (Three subspecies of the pupfish are designated as *state* and *federal endangered*: desert pupfish, Owens pupfish, and Cottonball Marsh pupfish; four are *species of special concern*: Amargosa pupfish, Saratoga Springs pupfish, Shoshone pupfish, and Salt Creek pupfish; one subspecies is extinct, the Tecopa pupfish.)

Pupfish range in size from one to two-and-a-half inches.

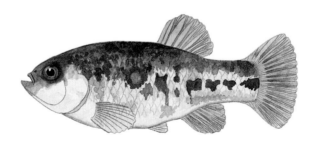

Pacific Lamprey (top), Owens Pupfish (bottom).

Sculpin
Cottus ssp.
(Native; see below for status of some species of sculpin.)

The sculpin is a small, bottom-dwelling fish. It possesses a flattened head, a large mouth, thin tapering body, and large pectoral fins. The eyes are located high on the head. There are seven freshwater subspecies; some are rare, others are numerous. The absence of a swim bladder allows them to stay on the bottom of fast moving streams where they feed and constitute prime sources of food for large trout. The prickly sculpin is the most widely distributed of the freshwater sculpins in California. (The rough sculpin is *state endangered*; the big eye marbled sculpin and reticulate sculpin are *species of special concern*.)

The sculpin seldom exceeds four inches in length.

Speckled Dace
Rhinichthys osculus
(Native)

The speckled dace is a small, slender minnow with a small mouth slightly under a pointed nose. It has a stout tail and small scales. It possesses dark blotches on the side. The speckled dace is the only California native fish found in all five fish provinces, and is the most widely distributed fish west of the Rockies. To avoid its predators, it forages for its food during non-daylight times, and hides among the bottom rocks during the day. (There are three subspecies that are *species of special concern*: Amargosa Canyon speckled dace, Santa Ana speckled dace, and Owens speckled dace.)

The speckled dace rarely exceeds three inches in length.

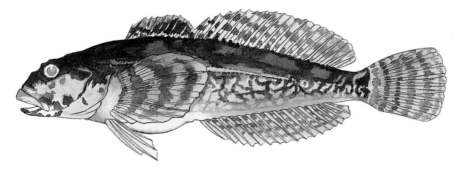

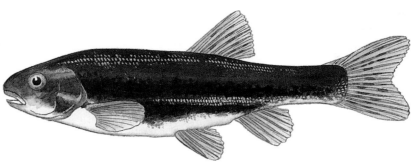

Prickly Sculpin (top), Speckled Dace (bottom).

Pikeminnow (Squawfish)*
Ptychocheilus grandis
(Native)

The pikeminnow looks like a pike but with a toothless mouth. It does have long and sharp throat teeth, however. Its color is olive or brownish green on its upper body to silvery on its underside. A predator fish capable of growing up to three feet, this sleek bodied native minnow species, once it matures, preys on most fishes, including salmonids. Although pikeminnow do not generally thrive in colder trout streams, they will opportunistically feed on young trout and salmon behind diversion dams. Where pikeminnow have been introduced beyond their native waters, they've had very detrimental effects on steelhead runs. One example of this situation is the Eel River drainage.

The pikeminnow readily takes artificial lures, producing good sport, although its stamina is shortlived. Its white flesh is bony but tasty (especially when smoked). A relative of carp and hardheads, pikeminnow occupy the waterways and lakes throughout the Central Valley, the Russian River, the streams feeding Monterey Bay, and warmer sections of mountain rivers.

In California the pikeminnow can reach three feet in length, although most specimens hooked by anglers will be in the twelve-to-eighteen-inch range. (The Colorado pikeminnow, no longer found in California but still surviving elsewhere, can grow in excess of six feet.)

*Note: The name of this species has recently been changed from "squawfish" to "pikeminnow."

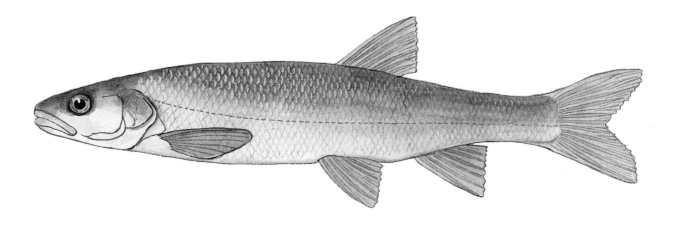

Pikeminnow (Sacramento Squawfish).

Sucker
Catostomus occidentalis
(Native; see below for the status of the species of suckers.)

California is home to eleven species of suckers, all possessing similar features and characteristics. Some are scarce, some numerous. Their dominant feature is the inferior or downward-facing mouth capable of sucking food from the bottom of waterways, often the same as those occupied by trout. Some species like the Sacramento sucker grow large, are strong swimmers, and will strongly resist when hooked, although they will not readily take bait or a lure. This sucker is very abundant in the Sacramento-San Joaquin drainage.

(Of the sucker species, four are *state* and *federal endangered*: shortnose sucker, razorback, Lost River sucker, and Modoc sucker; four are *species of special concern*: Owens sucker, Santa Ana sucker, Mountain sucker, Klamath large scale sucker; the remaining three species—Sacramento sucker, Tahoe sucker, and Klamath small scale sucker—are not declining species.)

Species of suckers range in size from seven inches (Santa Ana sucker) to the forty-inch razorback sucker. The Sacramento sucker can reach lengths of twenty inches.

Sacramento Sucker.

Splittail
Pogonichthys macrolepidotus
(Native; federally threatened)

The splittail is a large-scaled minnow with a small head and one barbel on each end of the upper jaw. The upper lobe of the caudal fin is noticeably longer than the lower one. Splittail are primarily freshwater fish, but are tolerant of moderate salinity. They are sought as a food source by some groups, and as a bait source by sport anglers. Splittail have disappeared from much of their native range because dams, diversions, and agricultural development have eliminated or drastically altered a great amount of their historic habitat. They are now confined largely to the Sacramento-San Joaquin Delta where they are preyed upon by striped bass.

The splittail can grow up to sixteen inches.

Threespine Stickleback
Gasterosteus aculeatus
(Native)

The threespine stickleback is a small native fish prized by aquarium owners. Its name is derived from the presence of three separate dorsal spines in front of the soft dorsal fin. The pelvic fin consists of long, sharp spines the fish raises when it is threatened. Its body is covered with a few bony plates or shields in place of scales. Sticklebacks prefer quiet pools with abundant aquatic vegetation, backwater areas, and the slower sides of streams. They feed primarily on small, bottom-dwelling invertebrates. They travel in schools except when breeding. Unlike any other fish, the male stickleback builds a nest of grass and sticks (much like a bird's nest) stuck together by a gluelike secretion. The nest, which the male guards, may be located on the bottom or concealed in holes, cans, bottles, etc. (The unarmored threespine stickleback is designated as *state and federal endangered*.)

The threespine stickleback is commonly one to two inches in length.

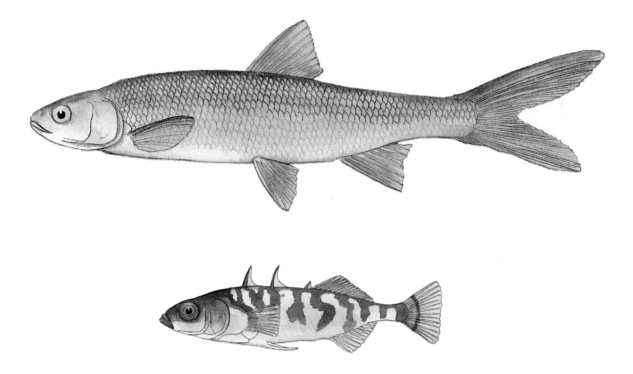

Sacramento Splittail (top), Threespine Stickleback (bottom).

Tui Chub
Gila bicolor
(Native)

The tui chub is a minnow found in slow moving streams and lakes, often traveling in small groupings, usually where there is abundant aquatic vegetation. Its head is large and conical, and somewhat flattened. The chub is the most abundant and widespread species in the native minnow group, and constitutes an important food source for large fish and birds. (There are many isolated populations of tui chubs structurally similar but distinct from each other, each *a species of special concern*, or already designated as *endangered*.)

The tui chub is the largest of the chub subspecies, capable of growing up to fifteen inches, but more commonly less than twelve inches.

Tule Perch
Hysterocarpus traski
(Native)

The tule perch evolved from a marine origin, one of the few freshwater species to have done so. It physically resembles sunfish, such as the bluegill, but it possesses a much longer dorsal fin with a distinct row of large scales at its base. Unlike sunfish, tule perch bear live young, a characteristic unique among California freshwater natives. It is somewhat common in the lower Delta, the Sacramento and Russian rivers, and Clear Lake. It is capable of thriving in small lakes and ponds.

The tule perch rarely exceeds six inches in length.

Tui Chub (top), Tule Perch (bottom).

Carp
Cyprinus carpio
(Introduced 1872)

The carp grows large, with twenty-pound specimens common. Its color ranges from silver to yellow, often with a brassy appearance. It has large scales, a humped appearance, and is quite heavy through the back. The upper jaw has two barbels on each side. A native of Asia, carp were introduced to California waters in 1872, and hailed as an exquisite food fish. But this reputation soon faded when the boneless and soft flesh of the fish became apparent, due in part to the water conditions here. Nor has it become a popular game fish in North America as it is in many other countries, although anglers will sometimes fish specifically for them.

Worldwide, more tons of carp are farmed for food each year than any other freshwater fish. The carp is the most abundant freshwater fish species, in terms of biomass, in the United States. In California, it dominates warm, shallow-water environments and has damaging foraging practices, often detrimental to aquatic species dependent on the environment. Carp produce large numbers of offspring, and grow to large sizes. One subspecies, the Koi carp, is used in ponds for its ornamental value.

The California record is fifty-eight pounds from Lake Nacimiento, San Luis Obispo County, in 1968.

Carp.

Fathead Minnow
Pimephales promelas
(Introduced 1953)

The fathead minnow is a small minnow, dark olive on top with tinges of brass behind the head and tan along the sides. Its distinguishing characteristic is a wide and blunt head. Breeding males possess small tubercles on their snout. The fathead minnow was brought from the East to California to serve as a bait fish. It has a high tolerance for high water temperatures, low oxygen, and organic pollution. Although legalized, it poses a threat to native fishes in stream pools and backwaters where it has been introduced.

The fathead minnow reaches lengths up to four inches.

Shiner (Golden Shiner)
Notemigonus crysoleucas
(Introduced (1891)

The golden shiner is a small, flat-bodied minnow with a greenish back, golden or silvery sides, a brass-colored belly, and large scales. Its lateral line is strongly decurved. The golden shiner is now the most popular bait fish in California, being widely commercialized for this purpose. Native fishes could just as easily have served the same purpose as the golden shiner, thereby eliminating its threat to them. Golden shiners illegally introduced to high mountain lakes by live-bait anglers often out-compete planted fingerling trout and ruin formerly good trout fisheries.

The golden shiner can grow to ten inches.

Fathead Minnow (top), Golden Shiner (bottom).

Western Mosquitofish
Gambusia affinis
(Introduced 1922)

The western mosquitofish, a native to the southern Midwest, was brought to California to control mosquitoes. A very small fish, it has a light olive body and dark-edged scales. Its tail fin is rounded; a very narrow dark streak runs along its sides. Having been introduced to most low and middle elevation waters, it probably is the most widespread freshwater fish species in the state. While it may serve an important mosquito abatement purpose in waters lacking native fish, it is unnecessary in waters where native fish that eat mosquitoes are found. It competes with or eats the eggs and larvae of native fish, especially pupfish.

The western mosquitofish grows up to two inches.

Threadfin Shad
Dorosoma petenense
(Introduced (1953)

The threadfin shad is a small, thin, silvery fish with a saw-toothed edge on the belly. A dark spot just behind the head and a greatly elongated last dorsal fin ray are notable. It was introduced into California in 1953 to provide a food source for larger game fish. It competes with native fish fry for zooplankton, and given the alien shad's abundance, the native fish may be the loser. It sometimes becomes so numerous that it interferes with largemouth bass production. It is also not compatible with the kokanee salmon, an introduced game fish.

The threadfin shad rarely exceeds eight inches in length.

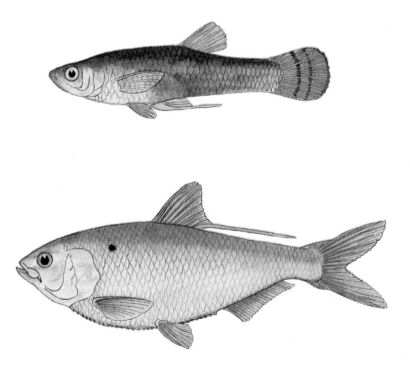

Western Mosquitofish (top), Threadfin Shad (bottom).

Acknowledgments

There are innumerable individuals working long hours managing California's freshwater fishes. Many of these persons are employed by governmental agencies, conducting their work in an era of diminishing budgets and resources. Nonetheless, many generously responded to the author's requests for information and materials, and critiques of sections of the manuscript. Bill Crary also was greatly assisted in his search for fish photos.

As this book grew in scope, Bill Crary and I discovered that the world of California's fishes is a complex and controversial one, and that conclusive information and definitive research results are elusive. We therefore need to state strongly that we alone are responsible for any biases, interpretations, judgments and errors that may be present in the book. That said, we both wish to extend our sincerest appreciation to the following individuals for their help:

E. Philip Pister (Desert Fishes Council), Rebecca G. Miller (Non-Game Fish Coordinator, DFG), Eric Gerstung (Threatened Trout Project Coordinator, DFG), Harry J. Rectenwald (Environmental Specialist, DFG), Neil Manji (Associate Biologist, DFG), Randall C. Benthin (Fisheries Management Supervisor, DFG), Stan Stephens (Wild Trout Biologist, DFG), Dennis McEwan (Leader, DFG Steelhead Project), Terry Jackson (DFG Steelhead Report-Restoration Card Coordinator), Richard A. Macedo (Associate Biologist, DFG).

Also, Christy McGuire (Fisheries Biologist, DFG), Betsy C. Bolster (Senior Biologist, DFG), David W. Kohlhorst (Senior Biologist Specialist, DFG), Curtis Milliron (Associate Fishery Biologist, DFG), LeRoy Cyr (District Fish Biologist, Six Rivers National Forest), Alexia Retallack (Information Officer, Conservation and Education Headquarters, DFG), Lisa Sims (Wildlife Biologist, U. S. Forest Service), Richard A. Bean (Independent writer and photographer), Ronald A. Iverson (U. S. Fish and Wildlife Service), Patrick Higgins (Consulting Fisheries Biologist), George Heise (Hydraulic Engineer, DFG), Ed Littrell (Environmental Specialist, DFG), Robert Kinkead (Independent photographer), J.R. Raymond Ally (Associate Fisheries Biologist, DFG), Jo Ann Rucker (Siskiyou County Visitors Bureau), Charles O. Minckley (U.S. Fish and Wildlife Service), Phil Baker (retired Fisheries Biologist, DFG), Dennis Maria (District Fisheries Biologist, DFG), Paul Chappell (Associate Fisheries Biologist, DFG), Anna Draper (Information Officer, Shasta Lake Ranger Station), Samuel V. Johnson (Senior Fisheries Biologist, Hydroacoustic Technology, Inc.), Karen Pearson, Yurok Tribe.

Sources

Behnke, Robert J. "Wild Trout and Native Trout: Is There a Difference?" *In Praise of Wild Trout*. The Lyons Press, 1998

Behnke, Robert J. "A Tale of Two Rivers." TROUT, Autumn 1998.

California Department of Fish and Game. *Warmwater Game Fishes of California*, 1965.

California Department of Fish and Game. *Freshwater Nongame Fishes of California*, 1964

California Department of Fish and Game. *A History of California Fish Hatcheries*, 1970.

California Department of Fish and Game. *Steelhead Restoration and Management Plan for California*, 1996.

California Rivers: A Public Trust Report. Prepared for the California State Lands Commission, 1993.

Cartwright, Wilbur. "California Hatcheries Offer More Than Just Fish." *Outdoor California*, July-August 1997.

Dill, William A. and Almo J. Cordone. *History and Status of Introduced Fishes in California, 1871-1996*. California Department of Fish and Game, Inland Fisheries Division, 1997.

Gerstung, Eric R. "Paiute Cutthroat Trout: Saving California's Rarest Trout." *Outdoor California*, November-December 1997.

Gerstung, Eric R. "The Status and Management of Redband Trout in California." Draft Report, California Department of Fish and Game, 1998.

Gerstung, Eric R. "Status, Life History, and Management of the Lahontan Cutthroat Trout." American Fisheries Society Symposium, 1988.

Gerstung, Eric R. "Status of Coastal Cutthroat Trout in California." *Sea-Run Cutthroat Trout Biology, Management, and Future Conservation*. American Fisheries Society, Oregon Chapter, 1997.

Lufkin, Alan (editor). *California's Salmon and Steelhead: The Struggle to Restore an Imperiled Resource*. University of California Press, 1991.

McGinnis, Samuel M. *Freshwater Fishes of California*. University of California Press, 1984.

McClane, A.J., *McClane's Field Guide to Freshwater Fishes of North America*. Henry Holt and Company, 1978.

Moyle, Peter B, Ronald Yoshiyama, Jack E. Williams, and Eric D. Wikramanayake. *Fish Species of Special Concern in California*, Second Edition. California Department of Fish and Game, Inland Fisheries Division, 1995.

Page, Lawrence M. and Brooks M. Burr, *Freshwater Fishes*. (Peterson Field Guides), Houghton Mifflin Co., 1991.

Retallack, Alexia. "Striped Bass; Revitalizing a Fishery." *Outdoor California*, July-August, 1998.

Sierra Nevada Ecosystem Project, Final Report to Congress, Vol. I, Assessment Summaries and Management Strategies. Davis: University of California, Centers for Water and Wildland Resources, 1996.

Steinhart, Peter. *California's Wild Heritage: Threatened and Endangered Animals in the Golden State*. (California Department of Fish and Game, California Academy of Sciences), Sierra Club Books, 1990.

White, Ray J. "Why Wild Fish Matter," TROUT, Summer and Autumn issues, 1992.

Index of Common and Scientific Names

Bob Madgic received a B.A. degree from Amherst College, and M.A. and Ph.D degrees from Stanford University. In his past career in education, he authored numerous publications, including an American history textbook (*The American Experience*, Addison-Wesley, Inc.). He is now devoting his time to conservation issues, and writing about fly fishing and the outdoors. His articles appear regularly in *California Fly Fisher*. His book, *Pursuing Wild Trout: A Journey in Wilderness Values*, was published in 1998 (River Bend Books). *A Guide to California's Freshwater Fishes* represents his ongoing commitment to informing the public on issues relating to native creatures and environmental preservation.

William L. Crary received an A.A. degree in art from Shasta Community College, and has devoted his entire career to the arts, working with oils, watercolors, pastels, pen and ink, and photography. As a practicing artist, he has focused on wildlife and landscapes, which are his main avocational interests as well. Through his art and his teachings about it, he hopes to raise awareness in others on the health of the natural world and what needs to happen to improve it. In *A Guide to California's Freshwater Fishes*, he combines his interests in the outdoors with his artistic talents to illustrate these marvelous but threatened aquatic creatures.